The Cistercians

M. Basil Pennington, O.C.S.O.

A Michael Glazier Book
THE LITURGICAL PRESS
Collegeville, Minnesota

Religious Order Series

Volume 4

The Cistercians

A Michael Glazier Book published by The Liturgical Press

Cover design by David Manahan, O.S.B.

1   2   3   4   5   6   7   8   9

Library of Congress Cataloging-in-Publication Data

Pennington, M. Basil.
    The Cistercians / M. Basil Pennington.
       p.   cm. — (Religious order series : vol. 4)
    Includes bibliographical references.
    ISBN 0-8146-5720-6
    1. Trappists. I. Title. II. Series.
BX4102.2.P46 1992
255'.125—dc20
                                              92-17175
                                                CIP

In gratitude to

Dom Edmund Futterer, O.C.S.O.

Dom Thomas Keating, O.C.S.O.

and
all the monks of

Saint Joseph's Abbey
Spencer, Massachusetts

Assumption Abbey
Ava, Missouri

and

Our Lady of Joy Monastery
Lantao Island, Peng Chau, Hong Kong

who have taught me and supported me in
the way of the Cistercians.

Contents

Introduction

No writing on the way of the Cistercians can say anything better than what is being expressed by the way thousands of monks and nuns in monasteries spread around the world are walking day by day this path of Gospel living. Spending a few days in one of these monasteries can lead one into a far better understanding of the way of the Cistercians, a deeper intuition into its meaning than can the reading of any number of books. The way of the Cistercians is a life lived. It is a day by day thing. And yet it is a transcendent event that comes all together in moments—all too fleeting, or so it seems—moments of what we call "contemplation," moments when God is God, and that is enough, that is all.

Words on a page can never fully capture this living reality. They may spell out the daily nitty-gritty. They may expatiate on the values that lie within these daily doings. They may point to or hint at the experience of what lies beneath the values: the reality that is ultimately only God. But they remain words, symbols on a page, trying to bear the burden of carrying a life across a gap of time and space from one living experience to another who may or may not be seeking to enter into the experience.

If all the reader is seeking is information, the words may suffice. In fact they may at times baffle, because they are trying to convey more than information. They are trying to convey an experience or rather invite the reader to enter into the reality of an experience. An impossible task—to convey an experience. In talking or writing about what has been experienced, we cannot convey the experience itself. It is incommunicable, unique—ultimately one's being in God, the God who IS. Writing about an experience to convey information seems a bit blasphemous. It is creating idols—images as far from the reality as is any idol from the living God. He is the only ultimate reality that gives all else sense because he is the source and ground of all others. All others are only in so far as they are a participation of his reality. An idea or a concept or an image that would pretend to be a complete or adequate presentation of an experience falls so far from the truth of the matter that it deserves to be called a lie.

A true way, a life, can only be known in its reality when it is experienced in the One who is the Way, the Truth, and the Life.

As the Cistercian Fathers, the great abbots of the Golden Age of the twelfth century, strove to speak of this way and write of it, opening it out for their disciples and sons, they were forced to come to a conclusion, one which they often stated: Those who have experienced these things understand what I am talking about and those who haven't—well, have the experience and then you will understand.

What value, then, is it for the non-Cistercian to read about the way of the Cistercians?

The Cistercian monk and nun, just as any member of the Christ community, follow a way, respond to a particular call or vocation for the sake of the whole Christ. It might then be of interest, comfort and even inspiration for other members to know more about this way of life lived by some thousands of sisters and brothers for their sake. This alone, this solidarity in Christ and even beyond Christ—if anything can be accurately said to be beyond Christ who lived and died for all to recapitulate all in his headship—solidarity in our basic humanness may warrant an interest in and study of the way of the Cistercians. If one's life by virtue of the interweaving of the common fabric as well as by the invisible yet powerfully active currents of grace is significantly empowered by the way these monks and nuns live, then knowledge of this way is significant.

But it need not end there: a significant thing worth knowing. The way of the Cistercians is basically the Christian way lived with a certain clarity and simplicity precisely because it is lived in a place apart which fosters a greater freedom to do what one wants to do, to be who one wants to be. The basic elements of the Cistercian life are the basic elements of every Christian life. Seeing them, being invited into the experience of them, can only invite you to enter more clearly and deeply into your own way as a follower of Christ and a human being concerned about the quality and substance of your human life.

Over the past two decades, since Vatican II, I have been asked on a number of occasions to look into new, experimental communities which were drawing their inspiration from the Cistercian heritage. Frequently I found that they were heavy on the externals but had little grasp of the inner reality. On one particular occasion I was asked to visit an Anglican community which had settled into a twelfth-century Cistercian tithe barn and was endeavoring to follow the Cistercian way of life. I expected it to be more of the trappings than of the reality of Cîteaux. But when, after only a half-hour there, I found myself with the superior standing in the middle of the garden talking about tomatoes and cabbages, I knew they were Cistercians indeed.

Cistercians are very down to earth people, very concrete and real. We have our feet on the ground, our hands deep in the soil of life. Contemplation, far from removing us from reality, rather makes us more fully aware of our oneness with all reality, and its oneness with God. For the true contemplative, all is God, all is prayer.

When Abbot Bernard of Clairvaux asked the novice master of his daughter-house (Cistercians call a house founded by another house its daughter-house and the founding house is called the mother-house) to write a manual for novices, Aelred of Rievaulx wrote on such things as finances, architecture, and music as well as crises and emotions and the transcendent and the cosmic. This is not because of some pseudo-spiritualism to be sure. The everyday real is very real and needs to be respected in its reality. At the same time, there should be no dichotomizing. The "spiritual" and the "real" are one. A monk's "spirituality" is expressed in and through the real. As the old monastic saying goes, you can tell how a monk prays by the way he sweeps the cloister.

The Pseudo-Dionysios, a fifth-century Syrian monk, has written a classic work on contemplation. In it he tells us there are three kinds of contemplation: direct, oblique, and circular. In direct contemplation, like Centering Prayer, we plunge directly into God, leaving all else behind, only, of course, to find it all again, and more truly, in God. Oblique contemplation finds God in and through his creation. Each thing that is shares in God's being and reflects in some way his truth and beauty. Circular contemplation circles around the many facets of God's being and truth, beauty and love that reveal themselves in our lives. Little by little we are drawn more and more into the whole and get some inkling of what the whole is like. This is the process of the contemplative life.

This seems to be the best way to look at the Cistercian way. Its richness and beauty are many faceted. We shall in this book look at them from various angles, hoping little by little to get more of a sense of the whole.

In the first part I would like to turn to Benedict of Nursia for my basic inspiration. The Cistercian reform of the twelfth century had this at heart: to live the Rule of Saint Benedict to the full. We will take a quick look at the history of the Cistercians to better appreciate this. Then we will consider what the Blessed Benedict saw to be the sign of the true monk: does he truly seek God. Benedict found this to be concretely expressed in three "zeals": zeal for obedience, zeal for a humble way of life, and zeal for the Work of God. An excess of this last zeal sometimes led to much imbalance in Benedictine observance, an imbalance the Cistercians sought to guard against by a wise balancing of the three elements: *lectio*, liturgy, and labor.

We will go on to take a look at how these elements are woven into the concrete daily program of the Cistercians today.

Finally we will look to the future by looking to the present: men going apart to become monks (Let me pause here for a moment to say that almost everywhere where I say "men" I could say "women and men" and where I say "monks" I could say "nuns and monks." I trust the reader will find it less burdensome if I do not), men being formed as monks, men finding their place in the Church as Cistercians.

I do not intend to spin out a lot of theory. There are many wonderful treatises on the Cistercian ideal. I will offer a bibliography at the end which will help you find them if you wish. And perhaps give you some assurance that what I have shared does have a solid basis in study and research. Nor do I intend to do a lot of intellectual exploration. I would rather speak from the heart, speak of what I know because I have lived it, what I love because it has revealed to me in the living something of its deep hidden beauty.

Words can be used to reveal only a part of the person, such as the professional words of doctors and lawyers. They reveal different levels and different dimensions, greater and lesser facets of the man, what he does, thinks, is. But there are deeper more personal words that seek to express the whole person. When they are spoken they leave nothing untouched, unmolded, unformed by the reality they express. It is this sort of words I would like to be able to speak in this volume.

It is important for us to have ideals. These are what draw us forth, make us stretch, keep us growing. It is only the intuition of an ideal that brings us to the cloister. But we are not long inside before we crash into the "real." And then we have a choice to make. We can cling to the ideal, rejecting the real, and spin off in an endless spin, looking for the ideal. Or we can let go of the ideal and settle down in the real and go nowhere. Nothing could be more dead. Or we can live that life-giving tension that clings to the ideal, keeping it ever bright and beckoning, and at the same time lovingly embraces the real, in ourselves and in others, and gently leads it toward the ideal. This is in reality the way of the Cistercians.

Lest all of this might seem to some too subjective a presentation of the way of the Cistercians I will include a number of documents. Some of these were written by the first Cistercians, those who first received from the Lord this charism for the Church. Others are the expression of today's Cistercians, still expressing the same charism for the same Church, but enriched by the graces and gifts of nine centuries of life under the Spirit.

May you find in this sharing of the way of the Cistercians not only a fuller sense of the richness that is to be found within our Christian heritage but also some useful inspiration for your own daily following of the Master who is the Loving Lord of us all.

Before concluding these introductory words I would like to express my gratitude to the monks of Saint Joseph's Abbey, Spencer, Massachusetts, Assumption Abbey, Ava, Missouri, and Our Lady of Joy, Lantao Island, Peng Chau, Hong Kong, who have welcomed me into their school of love where I have learned all that I share about the Cistercian way. I also thank Fr. Bede Lackner, O. Cist., for graciously providing the translations of the *Little Exordium, Exordium of Cîteaux*, and the *Charter of Charity* which appear in the appendices. May the Lord himself, through the intercession of the Queen of Cîteaux, reward them as only he can.

M. Basil Pennington, o.c.s.o.

Feast of the Assumption, 1992

1

What's in a Name?

I have often been asked: Are you a Cistercian or a Trappist? I have to answer: Both.

"Trappist" is in fact a nickname which belongs in the first place to the monks of the French Cistercian monastery of Notre Dame de la Grande Trappe. It was monks of this monastery who escaped the horrors of the French Revolution and, after long journeys, arrived in New York in 1803, bringing Cistercian life to North America. More important, the Abbey of La Trappe was the focal point of the renewal or reform of Cistercian life which took place in the century after the Council of Trent. Certain of the adopted observances were those which caused controversy among the Cistercians, dividing the order into two. The "war of the observances" as well as certain historical developments which forced the Cistercians in some countries to take on various active ministries led to the formation of two Cistercian orders. Toward the end of the nineteenth century, Pope Leo XIII had encouraged the diverse Cistercian congregations to come together as one monastic order. It was probably the commitment to various ministries more than a difference in observances which frustrated the Pope's aspirations. In the end the Holy See recognized two Cistercian orders: the Sacred Order of Cistercians now called simply the Order of Cistercians (O. Cist.) and the Cistercian Order of the Strict Observance (O.C.S.O.). The latter order, which includes the Abbey of La Grande Trappe and the congregation of monasteries that had formed around it as well as two other congregations of similar observance, inherited the Trappist nickname. The Sacred Order of Cistercians has sometimes been referred to as the Cistercians of the Common Observance.

Thus a Trappist is a Cistercian of the Cistercian Order of the Strict Observance. Cistercian nuns who belong to the same order are usually referred to as Trappistines. There are today over ninety communities of Trappists and sixty of Trappistines scattered across the six continents.

The two Cistercian orders share a common heritage, a spirituality coming from the Cistercian Fathers and Mothers of the twelfth century. The expression of this spirit is necessarily affected when a community is committed to an apostolate or apostolates of an active nature which generally engage the whole community. A few of the Trappist communities by way of exception are committed to certain apostolic activities beyond their own guesthouse. This is exceptional and usually does not mark the spirit or observance of the community as a whole. At the same time a number of the men's monasteries of the Common Observance and nearly all their convents of women are free from external apostolic activity. These communities follow an observance very similar to that of the Trappists.

I have always belonged to a Trappist community although by exception my own life has included a certain amount of apostolic activity not only in the monastic guesthouse but also outside the monastery. Thus while I will be writing primarily from a Trappist Cistercian outlook I am well aware of the effect of apostolic demands upon the monk living according to the Cistercian heritage. Such a monk can, of course, feel a deep kinship with some of the great Cistercian Fathers who, while they articulated the Cistercian heritage, often found themselves engaged in important apostolic missions for the Church—a reminder that the monk, no matter what his particular commitment, lives for the whole Church, the whole Body of Christ.

The differences between the two Cistercian orders do not lie wholly in the question of apostolates. In its directives for renewal the Second Vatican Council pointed monks and nuns not only toward their revered founders but also to their healthy traditions. The innovations at La Trappe in the seventeenth century, even though many of them have long since been abandoned, still strongly mark the life and spirit of the Cistercian Order of the Strict Observance. The struggle for authentic renewal for this order does lie in discerning which elements of this later reform and the developments that flowed out of it are "healthy" (according to the mentality of the Council) and are to be a part of the renewal and which are to be abandoned as betraying in some way the true spirit of the founders.

In a similar way, the later developments that led many of the Cistercian monasteries of the Common Observance to undertake educational and parochial activities must also be examined and regulated by a discernment of what is a "healthy" tradition in the light of the original Cistercian charism.

Efforts at such a discernment have led to the formulation of new constitutions for both orders. These constitutions seek to capture the spirit of the respective orders as they live their life in the Church today. We will benefit a good bit from these ongoing constitutional labors as we examine the way of the Cistercians.

2

What Is a Cistercian?

Early in the year 1098, an old man by any account, but for those times a very old man, Robert, Abbot of Molesme, age seventy, set out on a high adventure. This was nothing new for him. Ever since he entered the abbey of Montier-la-Celle as an enthusiastic and idealistic youth, Robert had been a seeker, a man who truly sought God, to use Saint Benedict's happy phrase, and a man who wanted to seek God according to the spirit and letter of Benedict's *Rule for Monasteries*. This led him to one monastery after another, to adventures successful and not so successful.

Indeed, it was success that defeated him at Molesme. When, after some years of struggle, he led the monks of Collan into the "hard and rough" ways of Benedict, and they began "to run in the way with indescribable sweetness," the fame of the abbey they developed at Molesme rapidly spread. The monastery was then blessed not only with an abundance of good candidates but also with many rich benefactions. The new-found wealth, or rather the care of it, soon had its effect on the way the monks of Molesme lived the Rule of Benedict.

Once again Robert longed for something purer, poorer, more simple. He was not alone in this. The better formed of his disciples, his prior Alberic, his subprior the Englishman Stephen Harding, and about twenty other devoted disciples were with him. Without counting the cost, Robert laid down the crosier of the rich and prosperous abbey and led these monks into the wilderness of Cîteaux.

Cîteaux, even though they called it an *eremo*, was not a desert in the sense we would usually give that word. It was not a particu-

larly attractive place, and it was far enough from the ordinary by-
ways of the world. The pioneers knew poverty and hardship as they
struggled to begin the New Monastery, the name they gave their foundation.

There was no intention on Robert's part to start a new order or
even a new monastic observance as such. He and his followers only
wanted to live the Rule of Saint Benedict with a certain fullness. By
practicing a greater poverty they hoped to keep themselves from
many of the entanglements with the secular society that land hold-
ing and benefices created.

These hopes seemed to be dashed to the ground when the bereaved
monks of Molesme obtained a papal command for Robert to return
to his former charge, and a good number of the monks of the New
Monastery opted to return with him. Alberic accepted the abbatial
crozier at the New Monastery, and the little community struggled
on. To insure the monks the freedom they needed to live the Rule
of Benedict to the full and at the same time save the monastery from
depending on outsiders, Alberic introduced into the Cistercian community committed lay men who took vows as lay brothers. These
men, fully members of the community, would take charge of the
temporalities both at the abbey and at its dependencies, leaving the
monks with the possibility of following literally the program laid
out by Saint Benedict. Alberic also fostered the development of a
scriptorium at Cîteaux to insure the monks with an abundance of
good material for their *lectio divina* (sacred reading). The fine illuminated manuscripts which we can see today in the municipal library
at Dijon bear witness to the fruitfulness of his endeavor. He also
encouraged those studies which would contribute to this, such as
Saint Stephen Harding's study of Hebrew and Greek to produce a
new and more accurate translation of the Bible.

When Alberic died in 1109, a holy and much loved abbot, it was
quite natural for Prior Stephen to be chosen as his successor. The
future of the New Monastery was still not very bright. Then in 1112
or perhaps 1113, Bernard of Fontaines arrived on the scene with
thirty of his illustrious relatives and friends, seeking admission to
the novitiate of Cîteaux. It was the beginning of a floodtide. Soon
the first band of founders went forth from Cîteaux to start another
community dedicated to the same ideals. Others followed. Bernard
led the third band to a "bitter valley" which he and his monks
changed into a valley of light, Clairvaux.

Each year the heads of the monasteries founded from Cîteaux would return to the motherhouse to take part in a formal meeting with the monks of that house. As their number increased, the monks of the local community took less part in this meeting, and it developed into a gathering or chapter of abbots whose concern was to keep their pristine ideal fully alive in all the houses. Stephen, the Englishman, set about composing a charter which would give form to structures that would assist the abbots in doing this. His first *Charter of Charity* received papal sanction in 1119. At the chapter of 1123 the assembled abbots formally approved the *Charter* and committed themselves to it, relinquishing some of their autonomy for the benefits of federation. The chapter of abbots and regular visitation of each monastery by the abbot of the house from which it was founded gave the local abbot the support he needed to fulfill his charge faithfully and lead his community in the ways of Blessed Benedict. This ratification of the *Charter of Charity* formally gave birth to the Cistercian Order.

Among the abbots who voted in chapter that day was the thirty-three-year-old abbot of Clairvaux, Bernard—a man whose reputation for holiness and wisdom was rapidly growing. His ability as a preacher and writer was also being recognized. It was Bernard, along with his disciples, William of Saint Thierry, Guerric of Igny and Aelred of Rievaulx and other early abbots, who gradually articulated a rich theological basis for the spirituality of the Cistercians. Perhaps nowhere is it expressed so succinctly and beautifully as in Bernard's letter to the monks of the abbey of Saint John in the Alps:

> Our vocation is to take the lowest place, it is the way of humility, voluntary poverty, obedience and joy in the Holy Spirit. Our vocation is to be under a master, under an abbot, under a rule, under discipline. Our vocation is to cultivate silence, to exert ourselves in fasts, vigils, prayers, manual labor and above all to keep to that more excellent way which is the way of love, to advance day by day in these things and persevere in them until the last day.[1]

A Benedictine

The *Little Exordium*, a primitive history of the founding of Cîteaux, emphasizes the great desire of the founders to live the Rule

[1] Epistle 142.

of Saint Benedict which they professed, their sorrow in seeing it transgressed, and their attempt to abandon everything that was contrary to the Rule or superfluous to its observance. The *Charter of Charity* required that the Rule was to be obeyed in all the monasteries of the new order in everything just as it was in the New Monastery. Regular pastoral visitations were to assure this.

Yet the early Cistercians were not literalists in their observance of the Rule of Benedict. They made some real adaptations to the social and economic conditions of the times, such as the institution of the lay brothers, the omission of deans and oblates, and the confederation of the monasteries. However, these innovations were directly ordered in their minds to a fuller living of the Rule. Their desire was to live the Rule of Saint Benedict integrally and fully. As Saint Bernard pointed out, the Cistercians "promised an integral, literal observance of the Rule rather than a life according to the Rule, since such is their interpretation of monastic profession."[2]

However, this statement, strong though it may be, must be understood in the whole context of Bernard's thinking. As he points out in the same book, the Rule was devised "because this manner of life was found expedient for the gaining or the preservation of charity"[3] Bernard, then, places the end of the Rule and of its observance in charity. In this he is clearly giving voice to the thought of Saint Benedict who expresses the same idea in the Prologue of his *Rule for Monasteries:*

> The good of all concerned, however, may prompt us to a little strictness in order to amend faults and to safeguard love. Do not be daunted immediately by fear and run away from the road that leads to salvation. It is bound to be narrow at the outset. But as we progress in this way of life and in faith, we shall run on the path of God's commandments, our hearts overflowing with the inexpressible delight of love.[4]

Again, in his chapter on humility, which is the heart and center of Benedictine spirituality, Saint Benedict points toward the goal of this

[2]*On Precepts and Dispensations*, no. 49, Cistercian Fathers Series (Hereafter CF), vol. 1 (Spencer, MA: Cistercian Publications, 1970) p. 141.

[3]*Ibid.*, no. 5, CF 1, p. 108.

[4]Benedict of Nursia, *Rule for Monasteries* (hereafter RB), Prol., 47–49, *RB 1980* (Collegeville, MN: The Liturgical Press, 1981) p. 165.

way of life: "Now, therefore, after ascending all these steps of humility, the monk will quickly arrive at that perfect love of God which casts out fear."[5] As a recent Benedictine scholar, Dom Pierre Salmon, sums it up: "In Saint Benedict's mind, all the observances it [the Rule] prescribes have no other purpose than that of preparing for the expansion of charity and union with God."[6]

The early Cistercians perceived the matter in no other way. The end of life is love. The purpose of a return to the Rule, a fuller living of the Rule, is growth in charity. Therefore Saint Bernard very logically concluded:

> It is right that what was established for the sake of charity should be omitted, discontinued or changed for something better when charity calls for it. On the other hand, it would be erroneous to wish to maintain contrary to charity something that has been established for its sake.[7]

That this primacy of charity is central in the spiritual heritage of the founders of Cîteaux hardly needs to be argued. The very name which they gave to our fundamental charter bespeaks it: *Charter of Charity*. And they themselves make it clear why they have chosen this name:

> . . . the mode of their agreement, it was charity by which the monks in their abbey, though separated in body in different countries of the world, would be indissolubly united in spirit. They had a good reason to name this decree the Charter of Charity because . . . it had for its object charity alone and the good of souls in regard to divine and human affairs.
>
> We wish to retain in the spirit of charity the care of their souls . . . that we may live united by one charity, one Rule . . . .[8]

This theme is common to the writings of the Cistercian Fathers, but it is most eloquently developed in the handbook for novices written

[5]RB 7:67, *RB 1980*, p. 201.

[6]P. Salmon, "Monastic Asceticism and the Origins of Cîteaux" in *Monastic Studies*, n. 3 (1965) 136.

[7]*On Precept and Dispensation*, no. 5, CF 1, p. 108f.

[8]*Charter of Charity*, Prologue and c. 1.

at the request of Saint Bernard by the novice master of the Abbey of Rievaulx, Saint Aelred: *Speculum caritatis, The Mirror of Charity*.

In establishing the primacy of charity the Cistercians have not sought to deny the importance to be placed on external observances, especially those outlined in the Rule of Saint Benedict. The Cistercians would not readily subscribe to a tendency which has been found in more recent centuries among some of the followers of Saint Benedict to spiritualize the Rule, to place all the emphasis on the inner spirit, maintaining that that is all that matters and giving little importance to the external. Here we have another element of the way of the Cistercians. A real importance is given to the observances of the monastic life and specifically to those of the Rule of Saint Benedict, since this is the Rule we profess. This attention to externals is a ready and realistic acceptance of the fact of each one's personal incarnation, that body and soul must work together.

Saint Bernard expressed it thus:

> I am not saying that external means can be overlooked nor that the one who does not use them will quickly become spiritual. Spiritual things are higher, but there is little or no hope of winning them or receiving them without making use of physical means. . . . The person in the best position is the one who uses both . . . harmoniously and with discernment[9]

Today in some areas of our life we need and have developed quite different observances, though in developing them we have listened to Saint Benedict's Rule and to our Founders' heritage of simplicity. It pertains to the way of the Cistercians that their life be wholly ordered to love and that there be observances in the life which follow on the Rule of Saint Benedict and are lived with a certain intensity to foster our growth in love. We are called to enter a Cistercian Christian community to live together in community with observances structured to foster a disciplined human and Christian freedom for a maximum response to God and to one another in love.

Another facet of the Cistercian spirit which is very closely connected with this central facet, the primacy of love, is the emphasis placed upon the experience of God. This might be referred to as mystical experience or the mystical element, but as the idea of "mystic"

[9]*Apologia*, no. 14, CF 1, p. 51.

has come to have many connotations, it is perhaps best for us to stay with the simple expression, the experience of God.

When Saint Bernard comes to comment on the central theme of Benedictine spirituality in his commentary on chapter seven of the Rule this characteristic thrust of the Cistercian way is much in evidence. For Bernard, Benedict's twelve-rung ladder leads directly to perfect love, to the delights and joy of contemplation. It leads to the chamber of the king where the soul "rests secretly in the king's embrace. While in this chamber the soul sees things that the human eye cannot see and hears mysteries that no tongue can repeat. . . ."[10]

This "mystical" element of the Cistercian way is nothing more than an explication of elements to be found in the Rule of Saint Benedict, the full flowering of the seeds sown by the Legislator of Monte Cassino. He would have his monks "run the way of God's commandments with an unspeakable sweetness of love,"[11] and "come to that perfect love of God which casts out fear."[12] He would have them "attain to the loftier heights."[13]

When our Fathers, the founders of the Cistercian Order, aspired to live the Rule in a fuller and more perfect way: *arctius, perfectius, pure, simpliciter, ex integro,*[14] their concern was not only and indeed not even primarily to live all its particular observances; their concern was to live the Rule in its fullness and to come to the fullness of the life of the Rule. A full observance of Saint Benedict's *Rule for Monasteries* for them and for us today means truly striving to attain the ultimate goal which the Rule of Saint Benedict sets before us, the perfection of love in the experience of God. In this way we seek an authentic living of the Rule we profess, in simplicity and poverty, in solitude and separation from the ways of the world. None of these elements is exclusively or uniquely Cistercian, but a balanced blending of them has produced and can still produce a monastic life that is eminently attractive and fruitful.

[10]*The Steps of Humility*, c. 7, CF 13 (Washington, DC: Cistercian Publications, 1974) p. 50.

[11]RB Prol. 49, *RB 1980*, p. 141.

[12]RB 7:67, *RB 1980*, p. 201.

[13]RB 73:9, *RB 1980*, p. 297.

[14]"more closely, more perfectly, purely, simply, integrally."

A Monk

Cistercians are Benedictines—Benedictine *monks*. Monk is the more basic reality, a basic human stance towards life, towards all reality. There are not only many kinds or congregations of monks within the Catholic and Christian tradition, we find monks among almost all, if not all the great religious traditions.

In some traditions monasticism plays a very important, almost central role. Monasticism is seen as being at the very heart of Orthodoxy. Mount Athos, the small monastic republic in northeastern Greece, is revered as the center of Orthodox spiritual life.[15] All Orthodox bishops must be chosen from among the ranks of the monastics. Among the Hindus, especially in India, the size of the monastic population is extraordinary. Monasticism is seen as the ordinary culmination of the human journey and, indeed, the only way to escape from the wheel of reincarnation and attain final and lasting bliss. Among the Buddhists, monks hold a most honored position. We see an expression of this in Sri Lanka where the front seats in buses are reserved for monks and even old women are expected to rise and give the monks their seats. In some Buddhist countries every male is expected to spend some time, however brief it may be, as a monk. In theory this acknowledges a deep reality and affords the opportunity for some intense spiritual training for life. In practice it too often becomes a mere formality undermining the real significance of monasticism. Be that as it may, monasticism is very present throughout the Buddhist world.

Among other great religions, like Judaism and Islam, while monasticism as such does not have a recognized place in their traditions, there are nonetheless groups that do incarnate some of the basic elements of the monastic way, such as the Sufis and the Essenes.

Over the course of the past few decades, I have had occasion to travel in Greece, India, and Japan, as well as in the United States. Wherever I went when I met monks of any tradition I was received not only with reverence and warmth but as a brother, one with them in our common monastic identity. And I experienced myself as being at home in their midst no matter how different the culture and traditions, the theology and practice.

---

[15]See M. Basil Pennington, *O Holy Mountain* (Wilmington, DE: Michael Glazier, 1978).

Monasticism is essentially a response to a call. Or maybe something even more urgent than that; it is an inner compulsion: *Caritas Christi urget nos* (The love of Christ compels us). There is a demand deep within us, in response to some kind of an experience, to live a radical "yes" to what is ultimate. I recall one day hearing a brother monk respond to a truck driver who was making a delivery at our monastery. The driver had asked the brother why he lived the kind of life he did. The brother said he really wanted to find God. The perceptive driver responded, "You wouldn't be living this kind of life if you hadn't already in some way found him." There is at the root of a lived monasticism an experience that has called for a redirection. There is a conversion, *conversio, metonoeia*. In some way we know the goal of all human existence. And we know that it is and yet in some way is not yet within us. There is a tension. There is a need that calls forth a certain commitment.

The monk is one who is committed, almost driven, to be present to the ultimate meaning of life in such a way that we let go of and even renounce all that is not necessary to our doing this. The monk seeks the *unum necessarium*, the one thing necessary, the pearl of great worth—the greatest worth, the treasure of life. The monk seeks to concentrate all on this one single and ultimate goal.

The practice, which we have noted, in some Buddhist traditions, of every male spending some time in his life as a monk, and even more the Hindu traditions that see the monastic state as the ultimate for everyone, express the valid insight that monasticism is not only an expression of a basic human stance in life, but it is a dimension of every human life. Every human person seeks to find his true self, to be at one with himself, something that can be found only at the very center, at the ground of our being where we are in some way one with the ultimate Source of Life and come forth from that Source. The monk commits himself, usually in some public manner, to developing in an exemplary way according to his particular cultural and religious environment the deepest core of his humanness. He commits himself to an uncompromising search for God with the readiness to break through all the obstacles on the path to the Center. Our vows, our practices, our observances are the path.

The Hindu traditions see four basic states or stages of life: *Brahmacharya*: the life of student, living in celibate chastity under the tutelage of a guru; *Grhastha*: the life of householder, begetting and nurturing children; *Vanaprastha*: the forest life, a life apart living in a quasi-retirement; and *Sanyasa*: the life of total renunciation, the monastic life lived in its fullness. The young man has a time apart to prepare himself for life receiving not only information but formation. Thus formed the young man goes forth to appropriate and integrate what he has received in the way that only lived experience can enable him to do so. Years of maturation which are also years of opening up the possibilities of life to others prepare him to move on towards the appropriation of his own fullness.[16]

In recent years I have seen a number of cases where men have embarked on the Cistercian life and have even taken vows. Then they have left the monastic way, as we have usually understood it, have gotten dispensations from their vows and returned to secular life. After some years, in one case after a couple decades, these men have returned to the monastery to embrace again the life of the cloister, have again taken vows and are living happy, fruitful, and holy lives. Others have not made so radical a break but have rather taken a leave of absence, sometimes for quite a few years, only to return to embrace the life with a new, richer maturity. In the past such men might have been looked down upon as being in some way unfaithful. Today we might be more inclined to admire their courage in stepping out of the security and set ways of the cloister when they discerned that their faithfulness to who they are and to what they are being impelled by God's grace demanded this of them.

I do not want to denigrate in any way the fidelity of the young person who enters upon the monastic way early in life and continues steadfast on his course. A wise abbot often will see to it that such a man, once he has received his basic formation, is called upon to serve in ways that are life-giving and maturing. He may be asked to serve his brothers in the business end of things, necessitating not only being busy about many things but also making many contacts with the secular world and perhaps even undertaking a good bit of travel. Serving the community as guestmaster, a monk will be called upon to respond to Christ in many, many different guises. Or the monk might find himself sent to serve our sisters and their guests at one of our convents. After years of such service, he will perhaps be even more eager for the "forest" experience, more ready to embrace the completely radical renunciations of the true monk.

---

[16]See M. Basil Pennington, *Monastic Journey to India* (New York: Seabury, 1982).

Not all monks need to go through these different stages, at least not so pronouncedly. Today a certain number come to Cistercian life only after they have had some experience as a householder. Others do come with little or no such experience, yet the Lord seems to lead them directly into the most radical sort of commitment which they pursue unwaveringly with a great simplicity. Others seem to work things out in their own particular if not peculiar way which might be identified as a "mid-life" crisis. All need wise care and compassion.

Saint Benedict tells us that his Rule is a rule for beginners. We perhaps have to listen to this and not dismiss it as a modest disclaimer. But in every journey, even the first step must be guided by the ultimate goal. Benedict points to that goal, maybe more hinting at it than fully developing it and the whole way thereto. He urges us to look to the Scriptures and to the Fathers for fuller direction. The Cistercian Fathers clearly did that and have elaborated a very full doctrine for us. They have also left for us a rich lived experience. We see that the majority of Cistercians through the centuries have quietly worked things out within the common life of the Rule. But some, including most of the great Fathers, were called to years of more active service for the Church and for their communities. The Cistercian way has not been the rigid following of a rule but under a rule and abbot the creation of a context for life, monastic life, marked by its singlemindedness and the exclusivity of its goal, a life that sought freedom to live this way and to undertake the praxis necessary for it. All human persons are to seek the ultimate goal of human life, but for the monk this is the exclusive concern of his life: "all that is not ladder is ignored." We can find in the way monks of different traditions pursue their course certain common sociological features, certain doctrinal resemblances, and some religious common denominators, but there is something even deeper than all of this. Monasticism expresses an aspect of being human that is deeply rooted in human nature. It is this anthropological reality lived in an exemplary way that the Cistercian shares with monks of every tradition.

A Christian

Fr. Raimundo Panikkar has reminded us that "the monastic vocation as such precedes the fact of being Christian, or Buddhist, or secular . . ., or Hindu or even atheist." Logically speaking this is certainly true. We are first of all human and monasticism is a dimension of human life, more fully recognized in some cultures and religions, ignored in others, but always there. Monastic is the genus and Christian, Buddhist, secular, Hindu, these are the species— logically speaking. Perhaps we can even say anthropologically speaking, if we stay at the level of the natural science of anthropology. But not in actuality. Not according to a more complete anthropology, a theological anthropology, one that allows itself to be illumined with the light of faith, with the knowledge that comes from the fuller revelation that has been given to us in Christ Jesus.

Men and women who have been baptized into Christ[17] have undergone a radical transformation. They are no longer merely human. They have in some very real way been divinized, made partakers of the very nature of God, made one with the Son in a oneness that is beyond our comprehension and is in some way like the oneness he has with the Father within the Trinity.

[17]I do not want in any way to deny the reality of what Catholic doctrine has traditionally spoken of as baptism of desire according to which many, perhaps most monks of other traditions have also been baptized into Christ. This book is about the way of the Cistercians who are Christian monks and so I will primarily concern myself with them here.

3

The Way

This book is concerned primarily with the way the Cistercians seek their goal, which is the goal of all Christian life, indeed, of all human life as it is designed by God: intimate union with God in Christ Jesus. This is a union which was ontologically brought about, brought about at the level of being, when we were baptized into Christ. At baptism we were Christed, divinized. We were made partakers of the divine life and nature by being made one with Christ, in a oneness that is beyond anything we can comprehend.

In this Christing we did not lose our unique personhood. We had been made to the image and likeness of God. This imaging was brought to its fullness in our Christing. God is absolutely one. Yet God is three persons who lose nothing of their personhood in their absolute unity. When we come into our oneness in Christ, we come into oneness with the Father and the Holy Spirit in Christ the Son. So we come to have this unity with God like unto the unity that Jesus has with the Father. Yet like Christ we retain our unique personhood. This leaves us free. And in this freedom we are able to attain unity with God and likeness to God in Christ at another level, at the level of our human freedom, of the will. Jesus was always completely united with the Father in the Holy Spirit at this level. He sought always to do the things that pleased the Father. Having attained a basic ontological unity with God in Christ through baptism, it is for complete unity at the level of human freedom that we strive in this life so that we might not only be fully in harmony with God in Christ but that we might also be fully in harmony with ourselves, with who we really are, Christed men and women.

Through inherited and induced human weaknesses, which are indeed all effects of sin, as well as from the effects of the sin in our own lives we suffer a serious impairment of our freedom. In this state it is impossible for us to be a complete yes to God and to who we are in Christ. Only by grace and by discipline corresponding to the work of God's grace in our lives can we hope to attain to the freedom that will enable us to be a complete yes to God.

The way then is essentially the way of obedience, the way Jesus trod who was "obedient unto death, even to death on the cross." But for us to be obedient, to enter fully into the way of obedience, we have need of other elements which will discipline us, enlighten us and win for us the grace to walk in this way.

The way of the Cistercians then, just as the way of every Christian, has all these elements. They are "blended" in the Cistercian way according as they have been laid out by Saint Benedict in his Rule and developed and modified by the Cistercian Fathers and Mothers and later vitalizing traditions.

Walking In Obedience

Ausculta, "Listen, my son . . . ."—the opening words of the *Rule* of Saint Benedict are an invitation to the way of obedience. The Latin word for listening, *audire*, is related to that for obedience, *obaudire*. The obedient person is one who listens, for we must first hear what is the will of God in order to be able to do it. However, the obedient person not only hears, he acts, he does the will of God.

The Cistercian life is set apart from the activities of the secular world, from the places where many live and act and make their inevitable noise, so that we can more easily listen. The Cistercian way inculcates a love for silence and provides amply for it so that we may more readily hear the divine voice. The Cistercian way sees *lectio* with its full development into contemplative prayer as one of its basic practices for it is here that God speaks to us most directly, intimately, and personally. The Cistercian way allows for an abundance of gracious space so that the monk may listen to God speaking to him within himself, in and through his brothers and through all the wonders of God's munificent creation as well as through God's inspired Word.

"Speak, Lord, for your servant is listening." This is the attitude Cistercians seek to cultivate as we walk along our way. A constant listening to God in all the ways he can speak to us and call us forth, so that with all our heart we can say: Yes, be it done unto me according to your word.

We are, each one of us, a certain listening. We have a certain openness, a certain receptivity to all that comes to us, whether it be through the ears or the eyes or any of the other senses. The listening that we are has been formed by all the influences that have shaped us. Truth and right reasoning, both at the human and divine level, have been inculcated into us by parents, Church, schooling, society, television, reading, study, etc. These have also inculcated into us certain positions, attitudes, and prejudices. We have our own ideas, values, and principles. These filter all that we receive and they set parameters to what we do receive. Some of us have very rigid parameters and can hear little or nothing of what falls outside of our pre-established boundaries. Others are more open and are constantly allowing their perceptions to expand their boundaries so that they can hear more and more, allowing the goodness, truth and beauty of other persons, of other religions, of other philosophical traditions, of this whole wondrous creation to enrich them.

In contemplation, following the yearnings of our heart, we allow all our parameters to fall away so that the fullness of God can come into us and take us beyond ourselves, bringing us into the experience of the divine goodness, truth and beauty in itself and in all of his creation. Only the person who practices contemplation, who allows the Holy Spirit to act freely within him through her gifts, can truly hear and can be fully obedient. Everyone who has been baptized into Christ has been given these gifts of the Holy Spirit, has been given the Holy Spirit herself, is called to contemplation, is called to this kind of completely open listening, is called to be led like Christ by the Spirit.

The process whereby contemplation heals, frees, and opens us is usually a long one. All along the way we struggle to discern the will of God for us and how we can be a complete yes to him. One of the great gifts that is given to us in the Cistercian life is the good of obedience. God as it were makes a contract with us. If we commit ourselves to the Cistercian way, he will guide us through the Rule and constitutions, through the local customs and guidelines, and through the directives of our superiors and even of our brethren.

Besides his primary chapter on obedience, Benedict has a chapter on "Whether the Brethren Should Obey One Another?" The holy Legislator establishes a certain hierarchy of obedience, yet we can expect the help of the brethren in discerning the way in which God wants us to walk in the course of our daily activities and even at deeper spiritual levels.

In the opening lines of his chapter on obedience, Benedict employs the scriptural quote "He who hears you, hears me" that is perhaps taken out of context and given an analogical sense, in the way that the Fathers so frequently do. Although superiors in canonically erected orders are in some ways integrated into the hierarchy of the Church and given a certain teaching and governing authority, no one would claim they partake of the infallibility that is proper to the divinely constituted magisterium. Superiors can be off in the things they command. They can even, according to Benedict, command impossible things. Yet in the realization that "for those who love God all things work together unto good," the monk can believe that God can work through these commands to bring about his own divine purposes.

This does not mean that Saint Benedict sanctions blind obedience. Nor does he want blind authority. Benedict wants the monk to be completely open with his superior so that the superior has every opportunity to hear what the Spirit is working within the monk.

If nonetheless the superior does command something that seems unreasonable or impossible the monk is to do his best, with humility and gentleness, to help the superior see his difficulty. I use the word "seems" because, as Benedict points out, sometimes something will seem unreasonable or impossible to us but when, after representation, we are still expected to undertake to do it, we sometimes discover that our judgment has been mistaken. We discover that by God's grace and gifts we are able to do things we had always thought impossible for us. Our edges have been pushed, our parameters enlarged. Obedience can often open out to us new horizons, new understanding of ourselves, a new realization of the power of God's grace in our lives. But sometimes, too, God wants us and our superiors to learn by our failures, by discovering in practice that something that the superior has unwisely commanded is indeed impossible.

Obedience is very freeing. The Rule, the local usages, the directives of the superiors decide many of the details of life for us, details that could be executed in many different ways. We do not need to be bothered in deciding. We can simply follow along and give our attention to more important things, to God and the things of God. Even in more important things, where discernment is often difficult—God so richly endows us and so many possibilities are open to us—obedience can give us the quiet assurance that the assigned path is a good way to use our time and talents. For the person who truly loves God, wants only him and to do his will, great contentment and joy is found in walking in the way of obedience.

Obedience can be difficult at times. This usually arises out of our lack of purity of heart. We still are attached to our own ways, our own opinions. Or we lack faith. It is sometimes very hard to believe that God can bring about our full growth and development in the way the abbot chooses for us when we and the abbot see things very differently—when he comes across to us as being much too narrow and uptight or much too liberal or showing favoritism towards others or harboring antipathies towards us.

There is a story from the life of Dom Columba Marmion. Columba was looked upon as something of a model monk, and in many ways he certainly was. One day his abbot asked him what he found most difficult in the monastic life. Marmion, looking over the abbot's shoulder, said quite candidly: "You, Reverend Father." Sometimes we look over the abbot's shoulder because we find it so difficult to see Christ in the man. We have to seek our Master as it were standing behind him. If we honestly seek to walk in the way of obedience, we can be sure that our divine Master is somewhere about, guiding and ready to support us in our efforts to walk in the way he did.

A Humble Way: Cistercian Poverty and Stability

True obedience demands true humility. The person who obeys because he has an inferiority complex is not truly obedient. The one who obeys out of fear or human respect or because it is the way to be accepted and perhaps get ahead is certainly not truly obedient.

The context for true humility and true obedience is that proclaimed by the most humble and most obedient in God's creation, the holy virgin Mary:

> My soul magnifies the Lord
> And my spirit rejoices in God my Savior

For he has looked upon the lowliness of his servant.
Behold from hence forth all generations will call me blessed
For he that is mighty has done great things for me
And holy is his name.

Knowing who we truly are: the very image of God himself, we know that it is below our dignity to submit ourselves to any other creature. To obey another human person for that person's sake, to please him or to satisfy him or out of fear of him, is below our dignity. Only God is to be obeyed. We obey others only for the sake of God and only to the extent that they are expressing God's will for us. Obedience to human superiors always has its parameters. Their commands which contradict the divine law are no commands at all for us. Moreover as Cistercians we commit ourselves to obey only what is in accord with the Rule of Saint Benedict. In obeying superiors within this context we are obeying God who speaks to us through them as channels or sacraments of his presence.

Knowing our true dignity, we know that we are all gift. We have nothing of ourselves. It is God who has made us to his own image, who has endowed us with life, with gifts and graces beyond all measure. "He that is mighty has done great things for me."

In the face of this largess, if I truly know myself, I must face my own failures to live up to this reality. How little of my potentiality is realized. How poorly I have used my gifts. How little I really know. How miserably I have failed to live up to who I really am. It is in this context we can understand the way of humility plotted out for us by Saint Benedict in the seventh chapter of his Rule and eagerly seek to climb the ladder of humility:

1. In the fear of God to be constantly on guard against sin.
2. Not to love one's own will.
3. To submit to superiors in all obedience.
4. To hold fast to patience amidst hard and rough things for the sake of obedience.
5. To confess one's sins.
6. To confess and to believe that one is of himself unworthy and useless for everything.
7. To believe and admit that one is less than others.
8. To keep to the common rule of the monastery.
9. To keep silent till one is questioned.

10. Not to be over ready to laugh.
11. To speak few and reasonable words with a moderate voice.
12. Always to show humility in one's heart and in one's bearing.[18]

These steps, this chapter, has been seen to be very much at the heart of Benedict's Rule. It is the first part of the Rule that Bernard of Clairvaux commented upon when he became an abbot and writer. He rightly pointed out though, that one does not seek out a ladder or mount one if he does not want to get to something or someplace. Benedict's ladder of humility is to lead us to the freedom of the truth: the truth about ourselves, the truth about our neighbor and the truth about God—the contemplative experience.

Obedience and humility, poverty and stability are but means in the Cistercian way to that one goal: the freedom to be completely to God, united with him on every level of our being.

The Cistercians' poverty is very different from that of their brothers and sisters in the mendicant orders, such as the Franciscans or Dominicans. The Rule of Saint Benedict dictates that the monastery should seek to have within its enclosure all that the monk needs for his livelihood, all that he needs to live out his special vocation. Monasteries often have land holdings that only the richest of the rich could aspire to have. These can be part of the means that the monks use to gain their livelihood. They are more often there to help create an environment conducive to contemplation. Our heritage encourages us to build simple yet beautiful abbeys. Bernard took pains to give us a model of this in his second daughter-house. Fontenay stands intact today to continue to inspire us. Authentic, spacious beauty is there, an environment that uplifts, that leaves the spirit uncluttered, that fosters contemplation.

Monasticism is indeed a luxurious life. A relatively small group of men enjoy their own church, their own usually well-stocked library, their beautiful gardens and woods, an apartness from the roughness of the poverty of the secular city. Monasticism is a luxury, a luxury that the Church cannot do without if it is to be faithful

---

[18]This summary of the twelve steps of humility is found at the beginning of Saint Bernard's *The Steps of Humility and Pride.* Bernard of Clairvaux, *Treatises II*, CF 13 (Washington: Cistercian Publications, 1974) 26.

to the Gospel. Jesus himself defended Mary as she extravagantly poured out the perfume of her life upon him. As she chose "the better part," he declared that it would not be taken away from her. Far more extravagant than the lands, the buildings and the holdings is the reality that men and women with an abundance of gifts and talents which could well be employed for the good of the Church and the poor sit in the idleness of contemplation. Only deep faith can understand this kind of poverty, this freedom of the poor in spirit who can be so freely wasteful.

The monks' poverty is an individual poverty. We turn everything over to God through our communities, all the potential and all the assets of our lives. "Not even his body is his own," says Saint Benedict. We walk in that spiritual childhood that confidently expects that all our needs will be met by the Father through the father of the monastery. We let our talents be used in any way obedience would have, and we can be content and more than content to see them left to go fallow while we are left free to engage our deepest person in the pursuit and enjoyment of God in contemplation. Through poverty of spirit we seek to be completely free from all possessiveness both in regards to what we have in the way of endowments from the Lord and in regards to all that we use from the provisions of the monastery.

We can readily see then how the poverty of the Cistercian demands true humility and is an expression of it. Like humility and one with it, it opens the way to the freedom of contemplation, to that complete yes to God, the giver of all good things.

Besides our specific vow of obedience and our more general vow to follow the monastic way of life, Cistercian monks and nuns make a vow of stability, a vow to remain always a member of our particular community. This, too, demands humility.

For some, one of the most difficult decisions they have to make once they have decided to embrace the monastic life is to decide which community they will seek to join. Every community has its pros and cons. With an awareness of where they have grown up, their particular temperament, their gifts and talents and attractions, candidates will seek to find the monastery that has the most pros for them and the cons they can learn to live with in peace. This is not always readily clear. This is one of the reasons why most monasteries have various pre-novitiate opportunities, and all monasteries have a novitiate and years of temporary commitment. It is true that the common law of the Church allows for transfers. But transfers, except in the case of starting a new monastery or charitably responding to the pressing needs of another community, are the exception and should be. After reasonable discernment and years of probation, we make a lifetime commitment to this community, to these men and all who should join us. Other communities will always have some more attractive points about them. There will be within our own community, besides the men who really support us as brothers on the journey, men who are a real burden, who seem to block our happiness and growth. The truth of humility will enable us to see that we ourselves are not all asset to everyone in the community, that the community is offering far more assets than we are fully employing, that this is the school of love we need, the way of compassion. We have discerned and our discernment has been confirmed by the community and the abbot that this is where God wants us. In faith we embrace this and believe that God can and will through this community lead us to the fullness of life, love and holiness he wants for us.

Celebrating the Work of God

The monks' whole life is in its deepest sense a celebration. Every life is. Each is a triumph of God's creative love. We are an expression of that creative love. And it is that creative love we want to participate in and magnify. All human labor is a participation, more or less conscious, in God's creative work. There needs to be a time and place when we give voice to this, give voice to all creation in proclaiming and praising this wondrous work of our God of love. A monastery is such a place, a place that in a special way is set apart for this proclamation and praise. The monastic way of life is laid out in such wise as to give the monk ample time for such proclamation and praise.

A Labor of Praise

Opus Dei, the "Work of God," can refer to all the activities of God, not only the "six days" of creation described so poetically in the first lines of Genesis but the ongoing work of the Father to which Jesus refers: "My Father works until now and so do I." It can also refer to all the work we undertake with and for God. But for Benedict it has come to mean most especially that labor of proclamation and praise which the monk undertakes in celebrating the liturgical hours. In Benedict's estimation this is one of the most important of the monk's tasks: "Let nothing be preferred to the *opus Dei*." A sizeable proportion of the monk's day will be given over to this task or preparing for it. More important than the hours of organ and choir practice and the many labors necessary to put together the texts and music and to prepare suitable books is the preparation of the minds and hearts of the monks who are to enter into this celebration. In order to proclaim appropriately the wonderful works of the Lord and all his attributes and to be drawn up into praise we must know of them and know him.

Receiving the Word of God

All creation speaks of its Creator. The Cistercian, as he walks down the cloister and through the garden and out along the road as he goes to his daily task, lets each thing speak to him of the loving Creator who made it. Or he may be attracted to turn within, to "listen" to the greatest image of God in all of the creation, his own created and recreated, Christed humanity. As our Byzantine brothers would say, there is within each speck of creation a "little word" (*logoi*) of the Word at whose word all was created. In addition to all these divine communications, we Christians have a privilege, shared in part with our Jewish sisters and brothers: the personal revelation of our God who spoke in olden times through the prophets and in these latter times through his Son, Jesus Christ our Lord. This Word of God, the Sacred Scriptures, is for us monks a constant place of encounter with God.

Sacred Study is an important part of the monks' life. We are to love the Lord our God with our whole mind. We ever need to seek to enter more fully into the meaning of the revelation: *Fides quaerens intellectum* ("Faith seeking understanding"). We Cistercians have available to us courses in philosophy, theology, Church and monastic history, patristics and liturgy. In all of these we seek to hear God, to let all the workings of the human mind and all the doings of history be words of God. There is a tremendous richness of faith to be shared with those who have gone before us. But the study that is dearest to our hearts and most eagerly pursued is the study of Sacred Scripture. We remember how our Founder, Saint Stephen Harding, even in his mature years willingly sat as a student of a local rabbi to learn the Hebrew language so that he could read the Scriptures in their original language and could translate this for his brethren. Our scriptural studies will not end though with the knowledge of languages and the various tools of interpretation. With the help of the Fathers, we want to enter into the deeper meanings of the Scriptures, meanings that do depend on the literal or historical meaning but through which the Holy Spirit can speak powerfully to us right now, where we are and according to our present need.

During their first years in the monastery all young monks undertake systematic studies, sometimes in classes, sometimes under the guidance of tutors, in all the fields relevant to our pursuit. Later those who are called to the diaconate or the ministerial priesthood will follow the course of study prescribed by the national hierarchy. Others according to their gifts and attractions will be given the opportunity to pursue graduate studies in particular fields. Periodically courses, workshops, and seminars will be offered to all to help us continue to seek the Lord with our whole mind, to keep growing in our Christian culture.

Besides studies, formal or personal, each monk will devote a certain amount of time on most days to what is usually called "spiritual reading." This is reading of a devotional or inspirational nature, a faith sharing with an author which inspires us to live up to what we know. It does little good for us to know all about God and his call, all about the wonderful things he has done for us, if we do not respond to him in a proper response to them. We are sometimes drawn into an immediate response by our very studies. Other times the events of our life are enough to motivate us to a wholehearted response. But often we need this additional reflective reading to motivate us to integrate our studies into our life in an effective way.

At times this need may be quite general, at other times we sense it in a particular area. We know the theology of the Eucharist, but as we participate in the community celebration each day our spirits flag. The hours in choir chanting the office may become routine or even seemingly meaningless. We may be having our struggles with obedience or chastity or patience. We need the inspiration another can give us through spiritual reading. We must remember that this reading is more than simply a sharing of thoughts or ideas. The men and women who have written in faith, even if they are long dead, are now truly alive in God. As we invite them into our lives through their printed words, we also invite them to be present to us spiritually, to speak these words to us now in the Spirit, and to intercede for us that their words may become effective for us.

Lectio Divina

While our sacred study speaks to our minds and our spiritual or motivating reading speaks to our hearts and wills, in *lectio divina* properly so called we seek something else. We seek to be brought into the very experience of God. *Lectio* is much more prayer than reading.

We retain the consecrated phrase in Latin here—*lectio divina*—because a literal translation would betray its meaning and the traditional Latin phrase connotes a whole process, a rather natural process whereby the monk goes to God. When monks hear the word, *lectio*, or the phrase *lectio divina*, we hear the whole: *lectio, meditatio, oratio* and *contemplatio.* Each of these four words suffers in translation.

Literally *lectio divina* means divine reading. We have to remember that this phrase was in use through many centuries when many monks could not read. It rather has the fuller meaning of receiving the Word of God. This may indeed be through personal reading. Saint Basil required that all his monks learn to read. Benedict provided time for the study of the psalms and office texts, but this probably meant committing them to memory. When I was a young monk, we were still expected to commit large portions of the offices to memory. A monk's *lectio* could be recalling some of the texts he had stored in his memory. Frescoes, icons, and later stained glass translated the Scriptures into pictures to be read by the unlettered. All could read God in his wondrous creation, perhaps drawing a good bit of inspiration and guidance for this from the psalms that were regularly sung in choir.

In *lectio* properly so called we do not seek so much to enlighten the intellect or move the will. Rather through the words of the sacred text we are seeking a visit of the Word. We want direct and immediate communication with God. Traditional monastic usages laid down what amounts to a ritual for the monk entering into his *lectio*. We are to reverently take the text. In earlier days a book was something precious in itself considering the many sheep that died to provide the needed writing material and then the long hours of scriptorium labor it took to fill those pages with beautiful script, but the texts are infinitely more precious in themselves for they are the very Word of God. Having taken the text, we are to kneel and call upon the Holy Spirit who inspired the writer and who now dwells within us to teach us all things, bringing to our mind all that Jesus has taught. After this prayer we listen to the first words on our knees.

"Listen" is the right word here. We are deeply aware of the presence of God in his inspired word. At Spencer Abbey, and I am sure in many other places, two lamps always burn in the church: one before the tabernacle proclaiming the real presence in the Eucharist, the other over the Bible in the center of choir, proclaiming the real presence of God in his inspired word. Conscious of this presence, we do not hasten on to read a chapter or a page. Rather, after listening to the first words, we kiss the sacred text and then sit, quietly listening to the Lord until the next bell calls us to some other service. There is no hurry. If the Lord speaks to us in the first words, we rest with them letting them engrave themselves in our minds and form our hearts, calling forth a response and leading us into contemplation. As we sit there, we move easily from one to the other: *lectio, meditatio, oratio* and *contemplatio.*

"Listening" is an apt word here for another reason. I smiled the first time I read a letter of Peter the Venerable in which he tells a friend that he has not been able to do his *lectio* for some days because he has laryngitis! Monks of old, when they did their *lectio* read the text to themselves in a quiet voice—it had to be a quiet voice or you can imagine what a jumble there would have been in the reading cloister. This practice of reading aloud has its advantages. Engaging other faculties it more completely engages us in the reading. The words touch us at more levels and thus more quickly become a part of us, forming our minds and hearts and shaping our speech. We moderns tend to marvel at the way the Fathers weave one Scripture text after another into their sermons and treatises. *Lectio* has made these words and phrases as well as the thoughts of the Sacred Text the Father's very own. I find even myself frequently using words of Scripture to express what I want to say. It surprises me when my editors begin looking for quotation marks and citations. The words have become my own, and I don't think of myself as quoting in using them. More important, the words are there to invite us at any free moment to enter into the process of *lectio*. They are there, too, to guide us in our decisions and our responses to life. Through *lectio* we come to have the mind of Christ—to use Saint Paul's happy phrase.

If *lectio* or *lectio divina* has a rather special meaning in this process, so does *meditatio*. Today, if you speak of meditation, most older Catholics will immediately think of discursive meditation where the meditator draws upon a passage from Scripture and seeks to enter into it using thoughts and images, hoping to break through and experience what is within it. Younger people today, when they hear the word "meditation" usually think of something more simple, perhaps a mantric sort of thing like transcendental meditation or something more akin to what we mean by contemplation.

Neither of these is what is meant in this more traditional use of the word *meditatio*. A word or a phrase received in *lectio* is retained in the mind. It perhaps repeats itself quietly or is even repeated on the lips. Gradually it forms the heart. To use Cardinal Newman's happy phrase: a notional assent becomes a real assent. The conceptual idea, which we perhaps fully accepted in faith, becomes something real for us.

Saint Luke twice tells us that Mary "pondered all these things in her heart." We cannot really enter fully into Mary's experience. Here was this little girl—so it would seem to us, though truly a young woman—one of a people that had managed by God's special care to keep its identity through centuries of struggle and war, captivity and exile by its steadfast adherence to the reality that there is but one God, the Lord their God, Yahweh. And now this little woman is told that that God has a Son, and she is to be the mother of that Son. There is no way even Mary's mind could grasp such a reality. Rather she received the word in faith and let it be there forming her mind and heart.

There is an old saying: Every translator is a traitor. In translating a text into another language we always in some way betray something of its meaning in the original. This is especially true when the New American Bible tells us that "Mary thought all these things over." The word "ponder" is a good one. It comes from the Latin *pondus* which means weight. Mary just allowed these tremendous realities to rest in her mind, and like a great seal they bore down upon her open and pliant heart—soft as wax—and made their full imprint. This is true *meditatio*.

The response such meditation calls forth from us, from an informed heart, is *oratio*, prayer. There is perhaps less danger here of betraying translation, although for some prayer immediately means saying prayers. And that is very far from what we are talking about here. This "prayer" is the immediate and spontaneous response called forth by the *meditatio*. Actually prayer formulas are more truly *lectio* inviting us to *meditatio* so that they can call forth from within us true prayer.

Depending on the particular word given us in *lectio* and brought alive through our *meditatio*, our *oratio*, our prayer may be one of thanksgiving, praise, adoration, repentance, petition, or any other particular sentiment or combination of sentiments. When our response is total or complete, when we respond with our whole being, then we have contemplation. We are simply all there for God, and the space is open for him to be to us in any way he wants, in the way that he knows is best for us right now. We have both eyes, both ears directed toward God and not, as is usually the case with us, one eye on ourselves, one ear listening to our own thoughts. We are simply there, mind and heart given to God. We don't now give God our beautiful thoughts, our wonderful ideas, our feelings or emotions, the sentiments of our hearts. We give God our very selves, whole and complete—as whole and complete as we can at the time and by his grace. We want him to be completely free to give us himself in whatever way he wants. He might leave us seemingly sitting there like a bump on a log (How often have we left him that way?). Or he might raise us to the seventh heaven. Wonderful! More likely most of the time he will leave us in the dark with a longing, sometimes sweet, sometimes anguished, a longing for him. There are two kinds of love: love of presence, when the beloved is present to us. It is full of delight and quite complete. And then there is love of desire, when the beloved is experienced as absent (God, of course, is never absent from us, or we would cease to exist, but he does like to play hide-and-go-seek). This is the love that grows, reaching out with ever greater desire. This is why the Lord so frequently hides: that we may keep growing so that he can give himself to us more and more.

I like the word "contemplation." It expresses the reality well. "Con" means to be united with: confrere, consortium, communion. "Tion" tells us that it is an abiding state, not just a passing experience. "Templa" is the interesting root. For the priests of ancient Rome the *templa* was a segment of the heavens. They would watch the flight of birds through this particular segment to ascertain the will of the gods. In time the *templa* was projected onto the earth and became the *templum*, the temple where priests and people would go to learn the will of the gods, worship and seek union with them. In contemplation we abide with God and enter into union with him, coming to know and want what he wants. To use the pregnant phrase of William of Saint Thierry, we attain a *unitas spiritus*—a unity of spirit. God's Holy Spirit becomes our spirit, our spirit becomes one with the Spirit of God. In contemplation we experience if only in a passing way the goal of the Cistercian life, of all Christian life, of all life: the fullest possible union with God, oneness with God. This for our part is something that can keep growing as we attain an ever purer heart. This is the essential labor of the Cistercian life: to grow in purity of heart through walking in the Cistercian way so that we may have an ever fuller oneness with God in Christ Jesus our Lord.

The Divine Office

Inspired by the Psalms[19] though probably more by contemporary practice, Saint Benedict legislated that his monks gather seven times in the course of the day and once in the night for the *opus Dei*. The Saint's seven daytime offices or hours as they are frequently called did not include the celebration of the Eucharist. Undoubtedly this was ordinarily celebrated in his monastery, at least on Sundays and feasts, for he made provisions concerning it. Today, thanks to an evolution of doctrine and practice, which is indeed a *re*newal, daily Eucharist is a part of the Cistercian way as it is for many of our Catholic people. For this reason, to remain in the spirit of Benedict and not be overloaded with community prayer, the Cistercians have generally discontinued celebrating the office of prime. Our seven times in the day then includes lauds or morning praise, terce or the third hour (Roman time inspired the names of these hours of communal prayer. The Roman day began at sunrise. The third hour would be around 9:00, the sixth at noon, and the ninth near 3:00.) sext or midday prayer, none or the ninth hour, vespers or evensong, compline or the completing service and the Eucharist. As Benedict

---

[19]"Seven times a day have I praised you" (Ps 119:164). "At midnight I arose to give you praise." (Ps 119:62)—RB 16, *RB 1980*, p. 211.

further prescribed, we rise around the seventh hour of the night for vigils or matins.

Prepared by our *lectio* and *meditatio* we are ready to enter into the Church's constant hymn of praise that rises up from all parts of the earth night and day to thank, praise and worship our Divine Benefactor and to humbly implore the pardon and benefits we all need. Each of the offices, though, has its own element of *lectio* and offers an excellent context for *meditatio*. The psalms themselves which make up much of the offices can be a powerful *lectio*. On another occasion we might use their quiet poetic recitation as the space for *meditatio* or let their words, so pregnant, give voice to our *oratio* or simply rest in a deeper *contemplatio* as our well practiced lips move quietly along with the rest of the choir. In Byzantine monasteries only a few of the monks are expected to be reciting or singing while the rest are free to follow along as the Spirit moves them. Among Cistercians and generally in the West, it is expected that all the monks take part in much of the singing and the reciting of the psalms. Perhaps there will be further evolution here. There are always some monks, especially among the former lay brothers, who are attracted to a more contemplative participation in the prayer of the community.

Each of the hours of the office has a reading proportionate to its length; vigils and Eucharist have two or three. There is usually a pause after each reading to give the monks time to assimilate the reading and choose a particular "word"—if one has not been as it were given to us by the Lord himself in the reading—to carry with us as we go on in the office or go forth to our other labors. Sometimes when our personal *lectio* seems to be high and dry these readings at the office can speak powerfully to us. They can be the moment of divine communication. Other times we feel so full that they hardly get a hearing. No great concern there. They will be back again as the cycle turns full circle. Mother Church is like a good Jewish mama. She piles our plate so high with good food that if we try to eat it all we will surely have indigestion; we will not digest all that we are taking in. It is better to take a good morsel and chew it well. The Fathers of the Church have a good image for us here. They refer to the "clean animal" of Leviticus (11:3): the animal that chews the cud. Like this wonderful beast of the Lord, we are in our *lectio* to gather up the nourishment we need. Then we are to settle down and chew the cud—*meditatio*—until we produce the milk of prayer and the cream of contemplation.

The longer hour of vigils, with its repeated readings and its prolonged psalmody feeds us and prepares us for the deeply quiet hours that will follow when we can enter fully into *meditatio, oratio,* and *contemplatio.* The offices of lauds and vespers, more colored by the feast or the season and often closely connected with the Eucharist, bring us more into the liturgical life of the Church. The other shorter hours are moments throughout the day which invite us to come to him who refreshes to find support in our quest for constant prayer.

There are many ways in which we pray the psalms of the office. Some days when the Lord is powerfully with us working in us we have little need of the psalms. They are just so much background music while our spirit rejoices in God our savior or rests deeply in his love. It is also possible at such times that we might find that the psalms enable us to give expression to what we are experiencing and what seems so inexpressible. Other days we do not seem to be able to pray and again the psalms enable us to find words that give voice to our anguish. There are days when we just seem dead and we follow the words of the psalms hoping they will spark some life in us. We can always make the words of the psalmist our own and enter into them as best we can. We can also hear them as the words of Christ himself, who so often prayed these psalms, and let him now pray them within us and speak to us through them. We can also hear them as the words of the psalmist speaking to us about Christ our God and join with him in his prayer and praise.

We can sometimes find great support when we remember that this prayer is rising even now from all parts of the Church. We are not alone. We pray with them all, those in heaven and those on the earth, the saints and the sinners, some who are very dear to us and some who we don't even know, some who share the fullness of our Catholic faith and some who belong to other wayfaring communions (let us not forget our Jewish brethren, the Lord's own; even now some of them are bending their heads in prayer at the temple wall), the rich, the gifted, the humble, the very poor, the needy, the simple, the young and the old, men and women of all colors and nations, praying these same psalms in so many languages.

Our reach can extend back through the ages. We can join Jesus and Joseph and Mary, too, in the synagogue at Nazareth or in their home. We can dance in spirit with David. We are one with all the choirs of the past, every Cistercian who ever prayed the office, and the Benedictines, Carthusians, and Camaldolese, too, and the Canons and members of the mendicant orders. We are with the martyrs who prayed these psalms and sang them as they awaited their encounter with the beasts or the bestial gladiators, with the youthful martyrs of Uganda and with those like Archbishop Romero who prayed the psalms and came to unite himself more and more intimately with the cry of the poor until he died for them. What a privilege it is to pray the psalms, to utter any prayer.

Constant Prayer—Silence

Saint Benedict saw these hours in choir as very special moments, moments when the prayer of the monks as it were came together and shone forth as the prayer of the whole community in harmony with the prayer of the whole Church in heaven and on earth. No wonder he could say, let nothing be preferred to these moments.

But these moments will not be what they should be if they are not the gems set in the crown of constant prayer, if they do not rise up out of prayer and flow back into it, energizing it, deepening it, enriching it. The context for the office is a life of constant prayer.

Jesus has commanded us to pray without ceasing. Monks strive to fulfill this command. Our whole environment calls us to it. Our daily schedule is organized to foster this. The spiritual fathers and the brethren are there to support us in this.

Monks will often finger beads, inspired by continuous tradition going back to the time when the fathers in the desert would use little piles of stones to count or more truly to number their prayers, to let the motion of their fingers help them center their minds and persevere in prayer. The words of life received at *lectio* or at the office or from a spiritual father or brother or perhaps some favorite ejaculatory prayer might keep our lips moving, joining our minds in feeding our hearts.

But the monk, like every other son of Adam, has to earn his bread by the sweat of his brow. We have to attend to other affairs. So such explicit prayer is not always possible. Thus we seek another kind of deeper prayer that can go on constantly as we attend to other things and respond to our brothers and sisters.

Saint Paul reminds us that we do not know how to pray as we ought, but it is the Holy Spirit who prays in us. Let me digress a little here to come back to this from another angle.

God made us to share with us his immense happiness. God the Father and God the Son and God the Holy Spirit were ecstatically happy. We all know that when we are happy we want very much to share the cause of our joy.

At Assumption Abbey I had a wonderful little friend. His name is Diers. He is a purebred mongrel. I don't even know where he came from. But he found that the monastery is a good place to get fed, so he is "our" little doggy. Each day after Mass I would go out for a walk. When I come out Diers bounds up to me, jumps up on me, tries to kiss me, and slobbers my beard. Soon we are off bouncing down the road for our two-mile walk. Diers is a great little friend. But you know, when I am happy and I want to share my happiness, I wouldn't think of going out to the doghouse and sit down with Diers: "Diers, old friend, guess what?" No. I seek out a brother who can fully enter into my joy, who can think and feel and sense human joy. Now suppose my fairy godmother came along with her magic wand and bopped little Diers on the head and he became human. She would also have to endow him with human faculties so that he could think as a human and feel as a human and enter into human sentiments. Then indeed he could enter into my joy.

There is far greater distance between you and me and God than there is between us and Diers. However, God does not bop us on the head. Rather he dunks us into the water. Through baptism he made us partakers of the divine nature and life so that we can fully participate in his divine happiness. At the same time God gave us his own Spirit to be our spirit. And he endowed us with a whole set of faculties to enable us to see things as he sees them and share in his sentiments. We traditionally call these the gifts of the Holy Spirit.

However, there is another consideration. No one knows us as does God, our maker, and no one respects us as he does. He knows that the greatest thing he has given us is our freedom, because herein lies our power to love. And God is love. God will never force his way into our lives. "Behold I stand at the door and knock and *if* one opens I will come in . . . ." If we want always to operate exclusively at the level of our rational thoughts and images, of our feelings and emotions, God will let us. In contemplative prayer we learn to let go of our own thoughts and images and to open the space for the Holy Spirit to begin to act in us through the gifts. Once God knows that we really want him to act in us in this way his action will become more and more habitual. Even while at the level of our rational consciousness we are engaged in our daily activities, at a deeper level through the activity of the Holy Spirit, through her gifts, we are conscious of the divine presence and activity and responding to it. In this way we come to constant prayer, constant communion with God even in the course of study, conversation, and every kind of work.

Even though we can come to be able more and more to commune with God in the midst of the many details of life, silence remains for the monk not only a necessity but also something that is cherished. If I had a good book for every time I was asked about our Trappist vow of silence, I would have a mighty fine library. The fact is we Cistercians do not have a vow of silence. We do commit ourselves to live according to the monastic way of life and that necessarily includes a good bit of silence. Each monastery has its own proper agreements or guidelines in regard to silence. These generally include a great or night silence extending from after compline until sometime the next morning. During this time we agree to leave each other free to be to God, and we generally try to be as quiet as we can be if we do have to undertake any activity other than prayer during these hours. During the day hours there are usually places of great silence where we avoid conversation and noise as much as possible. These might include the church, cloisters, chapter house, scriptorium, refectory, and the monks' cells. There are other areas where we speak only what is necessary. This would usually be many of the work areas. We do need at times to talk in order to execute the work efficiently. But apart from that we like to leave each other free to pray as we work, insofar as this is compatible with the work at hand. Finally, there are the places where the monks speak freely. These are very important for community life and for the individual. We need to relax at times, and there are times when we need to talk to someone. The guidelines are worked out in such wise that the monk can find the silence he needs and he can find fraternal support in conversation when that is good for him. Different monks at different times in our lives need more of one or more of the other. The monastery which is set up to foster the life of each member seeks to provide for this.

Monks very much need silence to listen to God and to listen to ourselves, to read and study and pray. The recent adoption of private cells by the Trappists was in view of facilitating this. When a monk retires to his cell, he can usually count not only on quietness but that he will not be disturbed unless there is a real emergency. When he closes the door of his cell, he is in a place apart. It is his secret place where he meets the Lover and enjoys that secret time with him. It is the nuptial chamber.

There is not a great distance from *cella* to *coelum*, from the cell to heaven. But it is a step away from heaven. Hence at times it can seem a veritable purgatory, a place of purgation. In the silence we touch our emptiness, our loneliness, our longing. We are confronted with our infidelities and even in the silence tempted to be yet again unfaithful and to seek to escape from the silence and the solitude. But we know that it is here with a word or a simple movement of love we can cut through all this and reach in and touch God, often in purest faith without the least bit of consolation, yet none the less surely. A true monk's soul at times longs for silence. When obedience puts us to serving tasks, we have to beware of Martha's temptation to complain about Mary who is privileged to remain at the Lord's feet. That is good. As Saint Bernard well said, blessed is the monastery where the Marthas do envy the Marys and sad is that monastery—God forbid there ever be such—where the Marys envy the Marthas.

In the end the monk learns that God speaks by silence and can be heard in silence. And that nothing really needs to be said. Silence is enough.

And of Creation

In the powerful, poetic account of Genesis, God labored for six days, and he saw that all that he made was good, very good. Creation is certainly something to celebrate. And it certainly is not something that is over and done with. As Jesus tells us, "The Father works until now. . . ." In creating God does not labor as some carpenter who makes a fine chair, sets it on its four feet and walks away. The chair can do fine without the carpenter. This is because the carpenter made it out of something. God does not make us out of something. Nor does he make us out of nothing. Such a belief—that we are made out of nothing—certainly does not help us to celebrate the wonder of our being.

Do you remember the story in Saint Luke's Gospel of the rich young man who ran up to our Lord and asked him: "Good Master, what must I do to obtain eternal life?" Jesus, being a good rabbi, answered the young man's question with a question. It is good to abide in the question. We too quickly turn answers into pat answers and close down, oblivious of the wonder of all that is. "Why do you call me good? One is good, God." Jesus was, of course, inviting the young man to a leap of faith: You are God. But the lad was not ready for that. At the same time Jesus was setting forth a basic metaphysical or ontological principle: one is good, God. Only God is and is good, true, and beautiful. Everything else that is and is good, true, and beautiful, is so only to the extent that it shares in his goodness, truth, and beauty, in his being. We and everything else in creation exist because at every moment God is bringing us forth into being by sharing with us something of his own being.

Herein lies the power of our prayer. God has so willed that the way in which he will bring this creation forth tomorrow and the next day, the next moment, will be determined in part by what we ask. "Ask and you shall receive."

"The Father works until now" and he invites us to participate in his work.

Work

Through the activity of the Holy Spirit, through her gifts, we become very conscious of the presence and activity of God in all. As we work not only do we see God in ourselves, working in and through us, but we also see God in all that we work with and all whom we work with. It is he who at every moment gifts us with the creative energy, intellectual and physical, with the gifts of soul that enable us to conceive and put into execution the creative projects we undertake. At the same time it is he who is bringing into being, sharing his being, with the materials with which we are working. It is he who gives me the mind and the mental energy and will to create these sentences and the fingers and the physical energy to type them into this word processor. And it is he who is giving being and its wondrous power to this word processor and to the electrical energies it is using. It is a labor of love and joy and creation, a celebration within God's labor of creation.

Penance

And yet it remains a labor, and it shares in the curse common to the sons and daughters of Adam: By the sweat of your brow you will earn your bread. Our labors will always bring forth their thorns and nettles and we will be afflicted by them and tempted by discouragement and despair.

In times past monks often undertook most extraordinary penances. Looking back from our present perspective, we might wonder how healthy they were. They could all too easily become projects of the false self, building up the "old man" instead of bringing about his mortification and death. We know spiritual athletes sometimes got into unholy competition. Saint Bernard describes such feats with great humor in his *Steps of Humility and Pride*.

Yet anyone who has seriously sought to walk the way of Christian holiness knows the value of mortification in due measure. When I entered the Cistercians, we did have the weekly practice, outside of Paschal time, to "take the disciple." This meant that on Friday morning after vigils, we would go to the dormitory, strip to the waist, and while the superior prayed the fifty-first psalm, the *Miserere*, we beat our bare backs with small rope whips full of knots. I think the most mortifying thing about this exercise for me was not the beating but the ridiculousness of this little exercise in the light of the beating I truly deserved because of my sins.

The Cistercians have long since laid aside their disciplines. In general we are content with the penances woven into the fabric of every day. Saint Bernard's maxim is well-known: *vita communis penitencia maxima*: the common life, my greatest penance. The openness with which Cistercian communities welcome candidates with a very great variety of backgrounds does challenge each of us to be very adaptable and flexible, ready to let go of our own will and desires in order to be supportive to our brothers or sisters and obey our superiors. Monks like everyone else will know the heat and the cold but perhaps will not have the air conditioning or central heating that is commonly enjoyed in their area. We will continue to wear the traditional habit. We will content ourselves with the monotony of a meatless diet and maybe even the less than expert skills of an unimaginative cook who has only the available products of the monastery garden (Though most of us are painfully aware that in general we eat better than multitudes of our brothers and sisters around the world, and are better housed and clothed. This, too, can be a painful thing with which to live).

Nonetheless, Benedict does urge his sons at least during Lent to take on something extra: "Although the life of a monk ought at all times to have about it the character of a Lenten observance, yet since few have the virtue for that, we therefore urge that during the actual days of Lent . . . let us increase somewhat the usual burden of our service, as by private prayers and by abstinence in food and drink."[20] But he wants to avoid all unholy athleticism. So he requires us to submit our undertakings to our abbot. In that openness we see how little they really are. Little room is left for self-deception or pride.

In the creative part of our work, we have the privilege of participating with God in his wondrous work of creation. Through the penitential aspect we participate in Christ's work of salvation for we are called to fill up what is wanting in the passion of Christ. The monk's work like that of any other human being has its share of frustrations and failures. I can remember lying on my back under a cantankerous old tractor for most of the first good harvesting day we had had in weeks. And snowshoeing out to feed the beef cattle as the plow stood stalled in the middle of the road, snow drifts forming around it. A sudden power failure has wiped out pages of creative work on my word processor. There are days when nothing seems to go right and the humidity is 95 and the temperature 105, days when everything comes out wrong and has to be redone, and days when nothing seems to get done at all. We all know such days which are further enhanced by the human conflicts that all too often crop up in the midst of our common labors.

I do not think we will handle these well and sanctify them and make them efficacious by offering them in union with Christ's passion if we do not prize the worth of penance and self-denial. When we do truly prize the worth of suffering and the cross in the Christ plan, then it is inevitable that we are not content solely with what happens to come along in the course of our daily living and labor.

[20]RB 49, *RB 1980*, p. 253.

We want to do more and seek to do more. As Saint Benedict says, we come to love fasting (no matter how much we love feasting) and watching (no matter how much we love the pillow) and all the other exercises of the monastic life.

Among the last lines penned by the venerable Legislator of Monte Cassino are these final words of the Prologue of his *Rule for Monasteries: Passionibus Christi per patientiam participemur.* "We shall through patience share in the sufferings of Christ." We have to be patient with ourselves and with our neighbors and above all with God. As he told Isaiah so long ago: "My ways are not your ways nor my thoughts your thoughts but as high as is heaven above the earth are my ways above your ways and my thoughts above your thoughts." He does things in his own way, yet we can be sure that for those who love him all things work together unto good. And he takes his own time. In fact, God does not dwell in time but in the timelessness of eternity. Already he is enjoying the finished product, so to speak. Already he enjoys us in the fullness he shall bring us to when he calls us home to his kingdom. The first time I realized this I was not too happy with him. Here I was dragging myself around, lower than a bear's tail, and there he was already enjoying Saint Basil of Spencer. But then he reminded me of Matt Talbot whom he left lying in the gutter for eighteen years before he picked him up and made him the saint he is. For most of us it isn't that bad. The important thing is that in faith and trust we count on God to complete in us the work he has begun, that he will bring us all to life eternal. On the way it is our privilege to participate in the saving passion of Christ as well as in the wondrous creative work of the Father.

4

The Daily Program
of a Cistercian Community

We have looked at many of the elements that are basic to the Cistercian way. As we have, we have given some indications as to where they fit into the Cistercian day. It might be useful to look at that day as a whole and see how it usually unfolds.

When I was a young monk and first began to travel about our international order, when I visited another monastery I knew exactly what they would be doing and when and how they would be doing it. The layout of the monastery would be familiar to me, much the same as my monastery back home. We prayed together in our common tongue: Latin. And if I didn't know the local language, I could fall back on our sign language to communicate with the brethren.

The Founders of the Order in their *Charter of Charity* laid down a principle of uniformity that was quite literally observed by the Cistercians of the Strict Observance. Bernard's exquisitely beautiful monastery at Fontenay remained the architectural pattern with only those variations demanded by the local geography. Monasteries were laid out in quadrangles with covered cloisters encircling a garden. To the north was the church, to the east the chapter house (the chamber where the monks had their formal meetings) and scriptorium (where the monks studied), to the south the refectory, and on the west the lay-brothers range. The monks wore not only the specified habit of white robe and black scapular (white for the novices) and ample white cowl but even underclothes of a medieval pattern.

An horarium, determined in every detail and adjusted to the seasons according to the Rule of Saint Benedict, was provided by the General Chapter and of obligation in every monastery. Like the liturgical calendar, it suited the northern hemisphere and especially the more temperate zones. Christmas, the coming of Christ, came when the light of day began to increase and Easter with the bursting forth of spring. The pre-Easter fast came when the nights were longer and the work was generally lighter. The shorter offices and the richer fare of Eastertime accompanied the heavy spring labors. This worked fine until the Cistercians started establishing new monasteries in the southern hemisphere and in tropical heat. Fortunately this expansion coincided with or rather was an expression of a new outpouring of the Holy Spirit which was influencing every aspect of Catholic life.

The Second Vatican Council's call to indigenization and subsidiarity was heard by the Cistercians. The General Chapter of 1969 adopted a Statute of Unity and Pluralism. This statute (see appendices) sought to lay down an outline of basic observances within which the local community needed to stay in order to authentically incarnate the Cistercian charism. All were aware, as the prologue of the statute makes clear, that this was a provisional discernment, allowing the order time and space to explore more deeply how the supportive unity which our first Fathers sought to effect through the *Charter of Charity* could best be preserved in a now worldwide order moving with the Catholic Church to be truly catholic, something universal and belonging to all peoples and cultures and not just to those of France or Western Europe. After some years of study and experimentation, the *Constitutions of 1987* have sought to more firmly establish this new approach to Cistercian unity, fully accepting the universal Church's recognition that the order's more detailed statutes will have to be periodically examined and updated to meet the needs of the evolving times in which we live.

Within the context of this new spirit and legislation, we find a similarity in the way the Cistercian day unfolds in our monasteries throughout the world and yet there are some significant regional variations. The more recent foundations in the southern hemisphere have to respond to the fact that summer comes in December and Easter is in the fall. Tropical monasteries have to give due regard to the heavy noontime heat and to the monsoons. Diet and clothing will also be adjusted, but let us keep our attention on the horarium here. Again, I am referring to the Cistercian Order of the Strict Observance or the Trappists. Those Cistercians who have undertaken active apostolic endeavors have to adjust their daily life to meet the demands of their commitments to the People of God in their schools, parishes, and other programs.

Cistercian monks and nuns still arise "around the seventh hour of the night" as Saint Benedict has prescribed—around 3:00 a.m. This assures us of some wonderful, deeply quiet hours for prayer before the day's activities begin. The individual monk is usually free to rise earlier, and many of the older monks do, though younger monks are encouraged to get the sleep they need.

The office of vigils usually begins about fifteen minutes after rising. This usually consists of an invitation to prayer and praise, a hymn, some psalms, a reading, some more psalms, a second reading and a concluding prayer. On Sundays and feasts a scriptural canticle and a gospel reading will usually be added before the final prayer. Periods of silent reflection are interspersed throughout the office. In all, the offices might take thirty-five minutes or up to an hour or more, depending on the pace of the local community and the solemnity of the day.

Vigils is followed by a prolonged period for *lectio* in its fullest sense, a time for contemplative prayer. The length of this period varies from monastery to monastery. It is usually two to three hours.

Not long before or after sunrise (most communities no longer vary their schedule with the seasons as Benedict had provided and the former Cistercian usages required) the community again gathers in the church for the celebration of lauds or morning song. In most communities Mass immediately follows this or is integrated with it, the psalms of lauds serving as the preparation for Mass and the readings of Mass serving as the readings for lauds. Some communities prefer, at least on some days, to have Mass in the evening, often in conjunction with vespers. After lauds and Mass there is usually some time for prayer, *lectio* or study before the morning work begins. In most monasteries the monks are free to take some beverage with bread and perhaps some peanut butter or fruit at this time or earlier in the morning, whenever the individual finds it most useful.

Some communities prefer to pray terce before going to work, others prefer to keep it as a pause for prayer in the midst of work.

For this reason it is often celebrated by a community in small groups wherever it is convenient for the workers to gather. This office like sext and none, consists of a hymn, some psalmody, a short reading and a prayer. Saint Benedict had laid out a plan whereby the psalter was divided over the period of a week's offices. But the holy Legislator left it to the discretion of the local abbot to divide it in another fashion. Many communities now divide it into a two-week cycle.

At the conclusion of the morning's work, there is usually some time for a bit of *lectio* before we gather for sext or midday prayer. This office is usually celebrated in the church before the community processes to the refectory for the principal meal of the day. This repast consists of some soup, a couple of cooked vegetables, a salad, and some bread and dessert along with various beverages. In 1969 fish and eggs were added to the common diet, but meat is still reserved to the sick and to guests. Various pastas also add to the variety. Leftovers sometimes add to the selection available. Most monasteries have adopted cafeteria style for serving, finding this better meets the needs of the monks and considerably economizes on the amount of food used. Most monasteries today cannot readily distribute to the poor the food left over from the monks' table.

After lunch and dishes—even monks have to wash and dry lots of dishes, pots and pans—there is usually a period of an hour or so during which the monks are free to take a siesta or to employ the time in any other way they wish. For many it is a time for their hobbies: crafts, gardening, music, etc. Some enjoy a walk.

The celebration of the office of none, usually around 2:00 p.m., sends the monks back to work. Often this afternoon work time, though sometimes the morning work, is given to the young monks for their studies and classes. After the afternoon work there is time for some relaxation, exercise or other activity before vespers. Though the monk is free to spend the time in *lectio*, and many do, all are encouraged to get some physical exercise each day. Some prefer to take time for exercise in one of the earlier *lectio* periods and do their *lectio* now. There was a time when almost all monks were engaged in that kind of work that gave them sufficient physical activity so that there was little need for other exercise. But today with so much automation and administration, few monks enjoy work that demands much physical exertion. Running, jogging, and fast walking are the exercises most popular with monks these days. Some monasteries are fortunate enough to be able to offer swimming. Competitive sports are rather rare and are usually reserved to special community days, though some monasteries will have a regular Sunday afternoon game of soccer or volleyball. Such events are good community builders as well as healthy activities for the individual participants.

Automation as well as shifts in the economy of our societies have drastically changed monastic work. When I was a young monk, most of us would spend a lot of time out in the fields and in the garden from early spring until late fall. The garden work could be backbreaking, the field work very exhausting, especially when it was "extraordinary work," work undertaken in the evening when there was not enough time in the course of the day to get the fields ready or get the harvest in. Today a few brothers with modern equipment handle what a multitude formerly accomplished.

This, of course, is not true in all monasteries, especially those in the Third World, where this change in work has hardly begun. In the United States where agribusiness has so taken over and government subsidies so effect the economy, few monasteries have been able to continue with agriculture as their main source of community income. Today most monasteries have a small factory of some sort. Factories do not accord the kind of work most conducive to the balance and rhythm that best serves the Cistercian way of life. But such work does allow Cistercian workers to experience a certain solidarity with many of our sisters and brothers, giving some witness that such work can be sanctified and made part of a deeply Christian life.

Cistercians try as much as possible, just as our founding fathers, to do our own work and not employ lay workers who will inevitably bring much of the news and noise of the world into the monastic enclosure and will quite properly require of the monks all the care and concern that good Christians should bring to those who work with and for them. In poorer countries, though, it can be a great boon to the people if the monastery can provide employment. In which case we must be careful not to let such social services impede the primary reason for the existence of the monastery and the witness it is meant to give, and we must be sure that we do fulfill all the exigencies of social justice in regard to those whom we call to collaborate in our work. It is not always easy to find the right balance and maintain it. It requires a deep faith and conviction in regard to our particular vocation and its importance for the Church even in the Third and Fourth World. If the social situation is such that a community committed to a contemplative way of life cannot be supported, then the Cistercians should not go to such an area. It is the proper mission of others. But I wonder if a deep faith would allow us to exclude any area from our contemplative mission.

Let us return to our daily program.

Vespers or evensong is celebrated in the late afternoon. It is the other hinge of the day corresponding to lauds. It is a longer office. After the opening hymn several psalms are sung, usually also a canticle as well as Mary's *Magnificat*. The reading is also usually longer. And there are pauses for reflection.

In the pre-Vatican II horarium there were two periods a day when the whole community spent some time together in contemplative prayer. One was in the midst of vigils and the other after vespers. These periods are more and more commonly being restored to the monks' horarium. We, especially the young, feel need of the support that comes from being together in such prayer, giving this witness of faith and fidelity to each other. When the monks do all their *lectio* and contemplation behind their closed doors, this witness and support is somewhat lacking. While older monks might not sense much of a need for it, William of Saint Thierry points out that it is something we owe to our younger men who have a greater need. For this same reason some communities have periods where the monks are expected to do their *lectio* together in the scriptorium or some other common room.

After Vespers, and often before, there is some food set out in the refectory or kitchen so that those who want can get a light meal. Things are so arranged now that we can do as much fasting as we want, with the blessing of our spiritual father, without others being particularly aware of it. And we can get as much to eat and drink as we need. This time after vespers is again a rather free time for the monks. Some will go to prayer or *lectio*, others might find it a time to walk or talk with a confrere or to visit the sick.

Some evenings before compline there will be a class or lecture or community meeting or a chapter talk by the abbot. Before the changes the community gathered in chapter each morning after the office of prime for some prayers. Then we would listen to a section from the Rule and the abbot would give a talk. This was all discontinued with the office of prime. On Sundays most communities will gather after the office of lauds and celebrate Mass later in the morning (though some reverse this order) and the abbot will give a talk.

If he wants to give additional talks to the community—and most abbots do, the abbot will gather the community in the evening before compline. According to the Rule of Saint Benedict, the community gathered at this time for some spiritual reading. While there are some values to be found in a community sharing a book, and for these reasons we still have reading at the main meal of the day most of the time, Benedict was providing for communities where many could not read. Today most find private reading more conducive to their growth and prayer than communal reading.

Compline completes our day, although we are free to continue to pray and read in our cells as long as we wish, just so long as we can rise properly rested for the vigils. At the conclusion of the office of compline, which is celebrated in most monasteries exactly as Saint Benedict lays it down in the Rule: a hymn, three psalms, a short reading and a prayer, all done in the dark from memory, Cistercians add the solemn chanting of the *Salve Regina*, often in Latin.

This ancient hymn in honor of Mary is very dear to Cistercians. Tradition tells us that the original text was written by a monk, Herman the Little, in the ninth century. One night in the cathedral of Sphire, Saint Bernard was chanting the hymn with the local canons and people when he was taken up into ecstasy. When all other voices fell silent at the end of Herman's hymn, the saint went on: *O clemens, o pia, o dulcis virgo Maria*—O clement, O loving, O sweet virgin, Mary. From thence forth the hymn has been sung with this addition. However authentic be this story, it is with these words that the Cistercian monk moves into the night silence. In chanting the *Salve* we not only pay filial homage to our heavenly mother, thanking this good Mediatrix for all the graces we have received in the course of the day. We acknowledge, too, as does the shrine at the door of the church in the cloisters and the statue or window now illuminated in the sanctuary, that this is Mary's monastery, that it and all it contains, above all ourselves, belong to her. She is our queen—and our mother for we are sons of the king, intimately one with her Firstborn Son, our Lord Jesus Christ.

Perhaps it would be helpful to set out here the horarium of one Cistercian monastery which is quite typical. This is the daily horarium of Assumption Abbey, Ava, Missouri.

3:15	Rising bell
3:30	Vigils, *lectio*
6:30	Lauds, integrated with Mass, *lectio* or study
8:30	Terce, work
11:30	End of work
12:00	Sext or midday prayer, lunch
2:05	None, work
4:30	End of work
5:45	Vespers, community contemplative prayer, *lectio* (supper)
7:45	Compline

5

Adaptation to the Individual

The Second Vatican Council enunciated a number of principles to guide Catholics in ongoing renewal. One of them which we have already mentioned is that of indigenization, that the Catholic Church truly become catholic. Jesus expressed his teaching and revelation in a very simple semitic language. The Christian community struggled for centuries to find the most adequate way to express his teaching in the philosophical concepts of the Greco-Roman philosophical systems. There were many falterings, as heresy after heresy was detected and rejected. Gradually certain creedal expressions became normative. So much so was this the case that converts had virtually to become Greco-Romans in their thought patterns in order to become Christians. There were notable exceptions for the apostles did bring Christ's message to India and other Eastern areas.

Part of the indigenization process, an important part, besides the integration of liturgical song and symbol, is the development of theologies based on other philosophical systems which will adequately express the truths of Christianity in a way that is more immediately intelligible to peoples who are not formed by Greco-Roman philosophy. This need is being taken seriously in India, Japan, and other places. The need of it in the United States with its existential preference has perhaps not yet been taken sufficiently seriously.

This indigenization which applies to theology in general, also applies to the theology and spirituality of the Cistercian way. We can hope that our newer houses in the Orient, in Africa, and in other parts of the world will begin to illuminate our Cistercian heritage in new ways. We can hope, too, that the many communities in both

South and North America will face the challenges of their cultures in rearticulating the Cistercian way.

More has perhaps already been accomplished in the area of liturgy both in the Church at large and in our Cistercian communities. Less perhaps in the ritual which formed and shaped the Cistercian life as a whole. The very detailed usages that had us making so many bows and performing so many ritual acts to inculcate and express our monastic values have largely been discarded and little has been given us to replace them. This has led to a greater simplicity and I might say nudity in our communal life which opens greater space for the individual, leaves more room for contemplation and challenges us as individuals and as communities to be more creative and responsible for the way in which we supportively interact in our daily communal living.

The Second Vatican Council also enunciated the principle of subsidiarity which holds that what can be adequately handled by the more local community should be left to it and not legislated for by the larger body. Thus what the national conference of bishops can adequately handle the Holy See should leave to them and not regulate. And what the local bishop can adequately handle the national conference should leave to him. And what the local pastor can handle the bishop should leave to him. And what the individual can handle the pastor should leave to him or her.

The same principle applies to the Cistercian order and has been applied in good part in the new Canon Law and the constitutions of the order. The law for the members of religious communities in the Code of Canon Law of 1983 constantly determines that particular provisions are to be taken care of by the individual religious institutes, either in their constitutions or the statutes of the general chapters. The new constitutions of the Cistercians in their turn leave matters to the regional conferences or more frequently to the local community, respecting in this the fact that the Cistercians are a federation of autonomous abbeys. In his turn the local abbot, taking into account his particular role as both superior and spiritual father of the community and of the individual monk, seeks to respect the individual vocation, the way in which each individual member of the community is called to walk in the Cistercian way.

Obviously it is not an easy task to apply concretely these principles in practice. It calls for constant discernment. But they are there to challenge us and call us to deeper and more responsible Christian decisions.

Another principle applied by the Second Vatican Council to monastic communities has added a dimension to this question for the Cistercians. Applying the principle of equality, the Council called upon all monastics to discontinue any class system within their communities. The Trappists had actually already been looking into this question and were most prompt in response. Within a month of the close of the Council, the order received from the Sacred Congregation for Religious a Decree of Unification. Respecting acquired rights it allowed any man who had made profession as a lay brother in the order to retain his status undisturbed. At the same time it allowed all the lay brothers to decide whether they would like to enter more fully into the life of the choir monk. They could lay aside the brown habit and wear the black and white one, replace their cloak with the cowl or a white cloak, attend the offices in choir, vote in chapter, canonically change their status from lay brother to monk—any and all of these were open to all the brothers then in vows. For the future though, within the Cistercian community there would be only one form of profession open to the novices, that of monk. All would wear the same habit. All would have voting rights. However, the precious heritage of the more simple monastic life of the lay brother, which went back to the earliest days of the order, was not to be lost. It would be incumbent upon the abbot with the individual to discern individual vocations. It is now possible for one to be canonically a Cistercian monk and yet in the balance of the ordinary day live the rhythm of life that belonged to the Cistercian lay brother, a life that devoted longer hours to work and prayed with a simpler office. However the sharp two-category division is gone. It is indeed an individual discernment. With each monk the abbot is to determine the monk's hours of labor, his participation in communal prayer, how he will participate in the prayer of the Church.

For some this loss of the lay brother status within the Cistercian community has been looked upon with great regret and has been very painful. While all would agree that the social inequalities had to be left behind (and this is undoubtedly what the Council was calling for) not all agree that it was necessary for the Cistercians to eliminate a canonical structure that incarnated a beautiful expression of Cistercian life. The full impact of this is not yet experienced

for there are still many within the order who were professed as lay
brothers and still make the inestimable contribution to community
life that lay brothers do. When these are all gone, how that contribution will be supplied remains an unanswered question. In a recent letter to all the members of the order, the abbot general declared:
"What is wanted is a genius who can think out an up-to-date form
of what used to be called the lay brother vocation." One thing that
is very clear is that the Cistercian monk's life has been profoundly
affected by the change and will continue to be affected.

The new canonical arrangement places a greater burden of discernment both on the abbot and the individual. At the same time
it allows for a much greater freedom in following the Cistercian way.
A vocation can evolve. Different phases in a monk's life can be more
easily respected and provided for. Whether the new provision has
actually increased the spirit of equality within the communities is
questionable. There may have been communities within which the
lay brothers were not fully respected as equals to the monks. There
are perhaps still communities where clericalism is having some nega-
tive impact (our communities still do and will need to call some of
our members to ministerial priesthood). But I think for the most
part these would be exceptional, and where they do occur they are
seen for what they are: aberrations or infirmities that need to be
healed.

The present legislation for the Cistercian order allows the greatest
possible freedom for anyone who is called to walk in the Cistercian
way. It is true that the ones who apply this legislation are, like us
all, sinners with all their limitations and shortsightedness. So the fullness of this freedom probably does not exist in all our communities.
But I suspect that the greater blocks to evangelical freedom are in
most cases within ourselves rather than in the structures and in the
way they are applied. In any case, the law is there in the new constitutions to challenge each superior and each member to apply to its
fullest the principles of indigenization, subsidiarity, and equality with
a profound respect for each individual as a child of God intimately
one with the Child, Jesus Christ.

6

Hospitality

One of Saint Benedict's truisms is that "a monastery is never without guests." Nonetheless the code the holy Legislator lays down for the reception of guests is very exacting indeed. And with good reason, for the Lord himself has indicated that hospitality is of the essence of Christianity, one of the things we will be judged upon when he comes to separate the sheep from the goats.

Some of our Cistercian monasteries are more accessible to the poor than others. But all of them know the experience of the hungry and thirsty, of the homeless knocking at the door. Most of our monasteries in the First and Second World usually think of themselves as primarily providing for the spiritually hungry and thirsty. We have to be careful in our efforts to provide what we consider an appropriate environment for these that we do not indeed turn away the Lord in the truly poor. In his program for receiving guests, Benedict places much more emphasis on faith than on discernment. Each guest is Christ and he or she is welcomed with joy.

What about the freeloaders? I believe Benedict would see them as Christ, too. They certainly are needy, more in need of something to restore their human dignity than the material help they are seeking. It is easier to give the material help. It is a real challenge to give help in such a way that we affirm the Christ person in the other and help him to get in touch with his true dignity (I have been tempted to use the feminine pronouns in writing this chapter because I think we monks are even more apt to fail in our response to the women, even if they are fewer, who come to our doors, whether it is to seek material or spiritual hospitality. For some reason our American monks got into the practice of welcoming only men into their guest houses. Happily this practice is rapidly being abandoned).

Our new constitutions call for us to offer a generous hospitality. It is a fact that in our affluent countries our guest houses frequently end up being a source of income for the community rather than a place where we give out. That income enables us to respond to other appeals. The mail and the telephone bring many of them to us. And responding to them is a part of monastic hospitality in this modern age. It is another way in which Christ knocks at our door.

The fact remains, even in those countries where many poor come to the door of the monastery seeking material help, the majority of those who seek shelter in our guest houses come seeking the particular alms that they can best expect to find in a monastery: food for their hungry souls, drink for parched spirits.

As in all aspects of the Cistercian life, so in the area of hospitality there needs to be discernment and balance and practice of hospitality that lives up to the Gospels and the Rule and at the same time does not undermine the living out of the particular Gospel vocation that belongs to monks. Monks from the earliest times, like our divine Master, have been led into the desert by the Spirit, have gone apart from the demanding needs of society to be free to be attentive to the Lord in their special call. And people have always come, no matter how far out the monks have gone, seeking their help.

The Cistercian community attempts in part to maintain its balance by asking individual monks to take turns as porter and guestmaster, in the name of the community welcoming all who come. It is one of the more demanding services to which a monk can be called by his brethren. The one fulfilling it will always need help and support from his brothers: practical help, relieving him at times so he can have some time for rest and refreshment and contemplation; lending a hand when the number of guests is making the task too big for one pair of hands; support that appreciates the service that is being rendered by our brother, affirmation of him and his labors, understanding his weariness and his particular needs.

No member of the community wants to be unmindful of what is going on at the gate of the monastery, in the porter's lodge and the guesthouse. Not only do we need to help and support our brother in his ministry but we also need, very much in accord with our vocation, to embrace with love and prayer each Christ who comes to our door. Among Saint Bernard's earliest works is his *Apology*, a spirited defense of the Cistercian way of life inspired by one of his closest friends, William, abbot of the Benedictine monastery of Saint Thierry. It is full of humor as well as of wisdom, biting at times, which made it immensely popular in Benedictine and Cistercian monasteries through the centuries. In the first part of the *Apology*, Bernard praises most highly the many wonderful blessings that the Lord had poured out upon the Cluniac Benedictines. And then he makes a most interesting and profound statement: Beware my brothers. These things may belong more to me than to you. For they most belong to the one who most loves them.[21] It may well be a brother who never sets foot in the guesthouse who most fully embraces the guests with the love of Christ and brings to them the profound healing they have come seeking.

It is one of the great joys and consolations of the Cistercian way that we who as individuals are the poorest of the poor, having absolutely nothing that is our own and who enjoy the beatitude of the truly poor in spirit, can yet offer through our community a generous hospitality to Christ in his poor.

We offer our guests a place apart, a rest for their bodies and their spirits, a comfortable room, some good food, and spiritual food in the form of books and talks. We welcome them into our community prayer, sharing with them the Eucharist and the office, and the graces that flow within a community at prayer. We offer them an open ear and a listening heart and whatever we can of the wisdom that the Lord might have given us. It is important, too, that we share with them our precious contemplative heritage, teaching our simple traditional way to enter into contemplative prayer to find the refreshment which the Lord promised and we all so need. And we acknowledge their Christ-person, offering them the honor and reverence due to the Christ. Our constant prayer is that each one who comes to our door may go away from it refreshed, more joyful and more aware of his true dignity and that of each of his sisters and brothers in Christ Jesus our Lord.

Over the portals of the old gatehouse at Gethsemani Abbey, Trappist, Kentucky, there was inscribed in large letters: *Pax Intrantibus*: Peace to all who enter here. Often guests come to the monastery seeking nothing more than to be able to rest a bit in the climate of peace they find there. Years, indeed, decades of prayer washing over

[21]*An Apology to Abbot William*, IV, 8, CF 1, p. 43.

an area that has sought to exclude as much as it can the freneticism of an ambitious, production-oriented world, does produce an atmosphere that quiets and frees the spirit. A few hours or a few days in such an environment can be very refreshing.

Frequently, though, the guest seeks a compassionate, listening ear. In an all too busy world, a very competitive world where each is intent upon making his mark, few are the ears that are ready to really listen. The monk who has long listened to his own soul and has seen it more clearly in the light of the divine compassion, knows more deeply the good and the evil that lie within each one of us. To the degree he has arrived at a purity of heart, he can truly listen and be a channel of the divine love and compassion. To the extent he has come to know his own true self, discovering it in the eyes of the divine creative love, he can mirror back to others something of their own deep goodness and beauty as men and women made in the very image of God and infinitely loved by an all-caring and all-healing Savior. The ministry of the porters and guest masters, of the spiritual fathers or mothers of the community, is a quiet one, but it has been the channel of salvation for many of the pilgrim People of God.

The monastic guesthouse is also a place of ecumenical encounter. When someone seeks the hospitality of the abbey, no question is ever raised about his race or religion, about his economic situation, or his sexual orientation. Anyone who wants to come apart for a time to rest in the peace of the cloister is welcome. He is expected only to reverence the other guests and their shared space and not hinder the quest for peace and prayer. Thus the group of guests who gather and share prayer and conversation frequently come from various Churches and ecclesial communities, and even from synagogues, temples, and mosques. During their time in the monastic guesthouse, they have an opportunity to discover something of each other's honest search for and response to God. And in their prayer and sharing they give witness to those among them who perhaps are still on the road to faith or are struggling with a certain agnosticism. While the monastic community does at times formally welcome representatives, clergy, and hierarchs of other churches for dialogue and common prayer services, especially during the Church Unity Octave (January 18–25), it is perhaps the ongoing, quiet sharing among the everyday guests that is doing more to heal the rents in the Body of

Christ. Nowhere perhaps is this more true than in our abbey in Northern Ireland, Our Lady of Bethlehem Abbey, Portglenone, where Protestants and Catholics share a cup of tea on Sunday afternoons and discover they have more than their love of tea in common.

Cistercian communities located by design "far from the haunts of men," far removed from the city streets, can do little to respond directly to the plight of the homeless, of the street people, beyond their compassionate prayer and their support of the Catholic Worker and similar sheltering groups. But perhaps by the example of their open and generous hospitality and perhaps also by some judicious words of encouragement, the monks do encourage their guests who live in the cities to open their hearts and even their homes to the homeless, to the homeless Christ.

"I was hungry and you fed me. I was thirsty and you gave me to drink. I was a stranger and you welcomed me."

7

On to Another Century

As the twentieth century winds down, the Cistercians look to the future. Fully inserted into the currents of renewal so strongly alive within the Catholic Church, with new constitutions and statutes, with many inspiring leaders and large numbers of new members in various parts of the world, we are grateful to be a part of the Spirit-filled times heralded in by saintly Pope John XXIII.

Post Vatican II Expansion

Renewal did not begin with the Second Vatican Council. We can recognize currents leading into it in the renewal of scholasticism in the time of Leo XIII, his call to the Cistercians and other religious orders to regroup and experience a new energy, and his powerful and inspiring call to social reform. Pius X renewed the Eucharistic life of the Church giving a heart to the beginning of liturgical renewal. Monastic communities were opening up a new era in patristic and scriptural studies. A monk of Gethsemani who spent some of his most formative years in Europe and kept in touch, Father Louis (Thomas Merton), brought these currents into the American monasteries. But not he alone, for at least every five years the American abbots like those from every other corner of the world made the journey to Cîteaux for the general chapter and then traveled widely through the continent. In 1951 a powerful French abbot, Dom Gabriel Sortais, was elected General of the order. Under his leadership the chapter of 1953 made such sweeping innovations that the Sacred Congregation for Religious postponed the implementation of most of them until they could be ratified by a plenary chapter in 1955. At least the innovations seemed sweeping then. In the light of what was to come they now seem timid enough. The winds of renewal were blowing in the order as they were in the Church.

The rapid expansion of the order began in America during the Second World War when after almost a century of existence the Abbey of Gethsemani gave birth to a new house near Conyers, Georgia. By the time the Second Vatican Council opened, the three American monasteries of men founded in the last century had grown to be twelve. The Trappistines had also come to the United States to begin their expansion to their present five houses.

This expansion in the United States though was only a part of a much more fascinating and challenging worldwide expansion. In the past forty years over sixty new Cistercian communities have come to birth. Since the monastery of Our Lady of Koutaba was founded in Cameroon in 1951, fourteen communities of monks and nuns have been established in Africa. Ten have been started in Latin America since Saint Joseph's Abbey (Spencer) sent a group of monks to Argentina in 1958. New communities in Japan, Taiwan, the Philippines, Indonesia, New Caledonia, Australia, and New Zealand have joined the older communities of China and Japan to form a new Pacific Regional Conference. Francis Archarya, a monk of Scourmont (Belgium), has successfully established an indigenized expression of Cistercian life in southwest India. Another attempt along these lines has been undertaken in Galilee about twenty miles north of Nazareth. The most recent undertaking is the establishment of a small community of monks from our monastery in Israel who are seeking to create an oasis of peace in war-torn Lebanon.

New Constitutions

On January 25, 1959, the popular new pope, John XXIII, made his first journey "outside the walls," visiting one of the four major basilicas of Rome, that built over the tomb of Saint Paul on the Laurentian Way. This basilica is cared for by the sons of Saint Benedict. After a magnificent liturgy which the Pope seemed to thoroughly enjoy, the Pontiff joined the monks in their adjacent monastery for a cup of coffee. It was on this occasion that John XXIII shared for the first time his plan to call an ecumenical council and to revise the Code of Canon law. I do not think on that day anyone expected the council to amount to very much, which was certainly true of the Roman Synod which the Pontiff announced on the same day. But this saintly Vicar of Christ called upon the Father to again send down upon the earth his Holy Spirit and to renew the face of the earth. Renewal was beginning in true earnest.

The Cistercian constitutions then in force were a product of the canonical reforms inaugurated early in the century by Saint Pius X. Influenced too much by the secular codes of the era, the products of those times lost much of the theological and spiritual richness of Church's canonical tradition. Pope Pius XII, who as a young monsignor labored at Cardinal Gasparri's elbow as he elaborated the 1917 Code and who was indirectly one of John XXIII's mentors, agonized over this betrayal and knew that a renewal of true ecclesiastical law would have to come. With it there necessarily came a call for all the religious orders to rewrite their own respective constitutional and statutory laws. Old wine skins could not hold the new wine.

When the Cistercians first met at Cîteaux in 1967 to begin the task of renewing their law, there was considerable confusion. What was to be done with the age old Rule of Benedict and the Cistercians' own *Charter of Charity*. Was there to be a *New Charter of Charity*? Was the Rule itself to be edited and brought up to date. Should it perhaps be dropped as hopelessly antiquated, enshrined in the reliquary, and given about as much attention as the other relics kept there. Over the course of the years commission followed upon commission and chapter upon chapter. Proposal after proposal was rejected. Since the wiser minds at the Roman congregation advised that we move slowly, this was all to the good.

The renewal chapter of 1969 did take a very important step forward. After elaborating a Declaration on Cistercian Life, it replaced a large portion of the 1925 constitutions with a well worked out Statute of Unity and Pluralism (see appendices). This statute gave the communities the space they needed to move ahead and experiment in the spirit of the Second Vatican Council. There was hope that whatever constitutions were eventually elaborated would come out of a lived experience and not just be the product of idealistic theory. It was clear now that Saint Benedict's *Rule for Monasteries* would always remain an enshrined document not as some old relic but as the ever-living inspiration for the Cistercian way. And the deeper purposes of the *Charter of Charity* which its call to uniformity sought to serve would be served in a new way, better for our times, but those aims of our Founders would ever remain normative for us as Cistercians.

Finally at the first general chapter to be held outside of Europe, at Holyoke, Massachusetts, in 1984 a text was elaborated and approved. In the course of the next three years all the members of the order had an opportunity to experience it and give their feedback. In 1987 a more definitive text was perfected and submitted to the Holy See for approval (see appendices). In the spirit of the new times, this approval involved a lengthy dialogue between the order and the Roman congregation, a dialogue which concluded with the final approbation of the constitutions, June 3, 1990.

Cistercian Nuns

One of the most basic questions that arose in the elaboration of new constitutions for the Cistercian Trappists was in regard to our nuns. The first Cistercians, who sought the greatest possible freedom to be to the things of God, had no desire to become involved with convents of nuns. Yet many Benedictine nuns eagerly embraced the Cistercian usages and many sisters of the early monks became "Cistercian" nuns. From then till now the history of the Cistercian nuns and their integration in the order is confusing. Since the approval of the constitutions of 1925, the Trappistines form one order with their Trappist brothers. There is one abbot general and definitory (as the Cistercians call their general council) to serve monks and nuns. Every convent of nuns had a father immediate, an abbot who along with his community concerns himself about the well-being of this "daughter house." With the developments in the post-Vatican II era, communications between the nuns and monks have increased, the bonds have grown closer, and the nuns have participated more and more in the overall life of the order. Suggestions from Rome that the nuns establish their own independent order were not well received.

If the monks and nuns in truth constitute one order, should they then not have one constitution for both branches? Since 1925 they have had two, and the Congregation for Religious seems to want that to continue. In the elaboration, then, every effort has been made to write two constitutions that are one in their spirit and doctrine and that completely dovetail in their practical provisions.

I think most Cistercian monks will agree that fuller collaboration with the nuns in these years of renewal has been a great enrichment. There was in the teaching and expression of the first Founders a deep warm maternal element of which the nuns help us to get a fuller grasp. Perhaps no order in the Church is so blessed with such a close bonding of men and women as is the Cistercian order today. There is no "second order" among the Cistercians. The nuns belong fully to the first order, and it is the expressed will of the monks as well as of the nuns that there be complete juridical equality within the order as soon as the Congregation for Religious and Secular Institutes will allow this. In the meantime a rich and enriching complementarity magnifies the gift that the Cistercian way brings to the whole People of God.

8

Why Do Men and Women Choose Cîteaux?

Each year hundreds of men and women, young and not so young (candidates at Assumption Abbey presently range from 22 to 57), present themselves at our guesthouses asking themselves and us and the Lord: Is this the life for me? Of the many who come, some stay for a week or a month, some go further, but the vast majority in the end continue their search elsewhere. There is no problem with this. A place and space and guidance in vocational discernment is one of the ways in which Cistercian hospitality expresses itself. We can hope that the time spent in the monastery not only helped along the process of vocational discernment but helped the individuals to ground a deep and powerful Christian spirit that will enable the candidate to bring more to whatever vocation he or she ultimately discovers to be the right one.

Thus, temporary vocation has always been a part of Cistercian life just as it has been a part of that of every other religious institute. Men have been led by the Spirit of God to the monastery for a time as part of the ongoing journey. Some recognition of this was given in the past with the development of various forms of associate membership in our communities such as family brothers or, more canonically, oblates.

Family brothers lived at the monastery, usually somewhat apart from the community. A monk served as their spiritual father and generally watched over them. They collaborated in the community work as it was assigned to them. In some instances they were given a small allowance, otherwise all their temporal needs were provided. This form of participation in Cistercian life has largely passed away because of all the complications introduced by social legislation. It is generally better for us to deal with lay persons as regularly hired help even if they do live at the monastery.

Oblates are men who enter quite fully into the life of the community. There is a very detailed statute elaborated by the general chapter detailing their incorporation into the community. They have a couple years of probation before they make their oblation, and then it is usually a temporary oblation for a number of years before they finally make their life-long offering. In general oblates have lived very much the same life as the monks, the difference being they have neither the canonical obligations nor rights of the monks and lay brothers. It is more fully acknowledged now that they do have some acquired rights when they have made their oblation. This status most commonly was used for men who for some reason, often a canonical one, could not actually enter the novitiate and prepare to become a monk. Since many of the canonical impediments that used to exist no longer do so (such as illegitimacy) or are now more readily dispensed (such as a marriage bond where the marriage has evidently irrevocably failed), there is less need of this particular form of Cistercian life. However, it does continue to exist for those who are called to lead it.

Today, many of our monasteries do welcome men who acknowledgedly only want to come and live the monastic life for a period of time. Perhaps this new opening is a fruit of our dialogue with the monks of other traditions in which this has been very much the practice. In some countries, for example Thailand, it is expected that every young man will spend some time as a monk prior to going on to marriage. The period may be very short, only a couple of weeks or less, or it may be for several years. So too, in our monasteries. Men can enter into the community life for as little as a month in some of our monasteries. The ongoing duration is discerned in light of the purpose for which the man has come seeking to live a temporary monastic life. Some monasteries are very open and flexible in regard to candidates for this experience, like Assumption Abbey, Ava, Missouri. Others have very carefully elaborated programs for temporary monks, such as Saint Benedict's Abbey, Snowmass, Colorado, and New Melleray Abbey, Dubuque, Iowa.

Transcendent Desire—Environment

Why do most men seek out the Cistercian way whether for a time or for a lifetime? It is a bit of a truism that the reason why one enters a monastery is not always the reason why he stays. Today, with the excellent programs most monasteries have to help someone in discernment and to prepare him to enter the community, this is probably less true than in the past. Nonetheless, there are aspects of the life that can only be understood through living them over a period of time. The meaning they impart to life does make a difference and qualifies our choice.

Through many years in vocational ministry, both formally as vocation father of a large abbey and informally ministering in our guesthouses, listening intently to many, many men, the deep aspiration that seems to undergird their search is the desire for something more, a certain freedom from the binding of temporal goods and relationships, the clutching spirit of the "world." Just last evening a young man in a college seminary who was devoting his summer vacation to living the monastic life was telling me how he felt a certain dread in returning to the seminary, for there the details of social life and the many material things he has seem to grab hold of him leaving him unhappy and unfree. When Saint Benedict described the task of the novice master, he said this wise old man was to see if the candidate "truly seeks God." That is what I find. These men in some way have gotten in touch with the deepest longing of their being, their innate desire for God. We have been made with a mind that longs for all Truth and a heart that is made for an infinite Love. "Our hearts are made for you, O Lord, and they will not rest until they rest in you." In breakthrough moments one is able to silence for a moment the brainwashing of Madison Avenue media with all the phony wants it inculcates and hear one's true self.

A Cistercian monastery is a place of silence, a place where one can find the quiet to hear. A Cistercian monastery is a place of freedom, where all is ordered to free us so that we can listen and respond to the deepest aspirations of our being, we can truly seek God and receive the help we need to come into true freedom to do this with our whole being. Cistercian simplicity does not apply only to our striking architecture with its chaste unadorned beauty and our plain chant. A modest diet and a practical spartan wardrobe, along with freedom from radio and television and the distractions of travel and visits, all contribute to allowing the monk to cultivate through study, meditation, prayer, and work guided by obedience a mind and heart totally orientated toward God—true simplicity.

A School of Love—Teachers

As we have seen everything within a Cistercian monastery is there to point to God, to speak of God, to free us to be to God. The buildings are arranged to lead us always to the church, the horarium flows in and out of the Work of God, the brethren share a common goal and support each other in fidelity to their common goal.

When one first has some perception of the something more that is possible to him and that corresponds to his deeper aspirations, he senses the need of someone who understands this and will help him find his way. Everyone and everything around him seems to be caught up in a competitive quest for the greatest amount of wealth, power and prestige. To most the thought of giving any of this up to seek something less tangible is virtually incomprehensible.

Who can understand? Who can show the way?

The media have set some in prominence. Mother Teresa of Calcutta is one of them. When I visited her novitiate in Calcutta, there were over three hundred novices present. And that was only one of her four novitiates in India, not to speak of other parts of the world.

Cistercian monasteries stand apart and bespeak a wholehearted dedication to that something more for they are seen as having no earthly reason for existing. Benedict spoke of the life he outlined for his monks as "a school of the Lord's service." The Cistercian founders, intent upon the fullness to which that service is meant to lead, called their cloister a *schola caritatis*—a school of love. Benedict not only insisted that the abbot be chosen for the wisdom of his teaching but that he surround himself with assistants and especially have a novice master who can help him lead men in the ways of the Lord. When Saint Bernard, the wisest of the teachers who first enunciated the Cistercian way, called upon his disciple Saint Aelred to write a manual for Cistercian novices, he said it should be *The Mirror of Charity*.

Cistercians the day they enter the monastery become students in the school of love. Through the years they gain a certain mastery, though we all are well aware that in this school we are always beginners who have infinitely more to learn from our true Master, the Lord Jesus Christ. When seekers come to a Cistercian monastery, there are teachers there for them, not only the monks actually living in the monastery. We share in a wonderful living heritage. The Cistercian Fathers and Mothers, the great spiritual masters of the early days of the order, live today in the Lord and are ready through their writings, especially when they are heard in the Cistercian environment, to teach us today how to enter fully into the Cistercian way, the way of transcendent love, a way that responds to the deepest longings that God has woven into the very fabric of our being when he created us in his own image and likeness and incorporated us into Christ through baptism.

Supportive Community—Eremitical Vocation

The ready availability of good and loving teachers is certainly one of the attractive elements of the monastic way. But we all know only too well, it is one thing to know something, it is another thing to live it. The current fostered in our modern world is certainly not one that flows into God. It is powerfully geared towards the amplification of the false self, that fabrication made up of what we have and what we do and what others think of us. When we perceive a deeper meaning to our life and want to pursue that, we have set ourself upon a very challenging course. It is in all truth swimming against the current, a very powerful current, and unfortunately a current that is not only outside us, all around us, but also even within us. Whether the candidate is 22 or 42 or 62, he has been deeply infected by the spirit of the world in which he grew up. The false self has had ample opportunity to grow strong within him.

To enter into an environment which eliminates much of the external force of a materialistic world is already a great help. But the one thing the monk can not leave outside the door when he enters a monastery is himself. His struggle will continue within the cloister. It is here where he is greatly aided by the help not only of wise spiritual fathers who can teach the way but brothers who can walk shoulder to shoulder with him along the way. Our weak faith is greatly supported when we see so many fine men, men often of very great capability, walking resolutely in this way and finding great joy in it. This witness of faith is very supportive. Our practice is so much easier when it is the common practice. So often I have been told by some visitor: I could never get up at 3:00 in the morning. Neither could I if I had to do it on my own while all the world around me slept blissfully on. But when all around me are rising at that time and hastening to the church to praise the Lord, I can hardly rest abed. So too for the silence, the fasting, the constant prayer. "When a brother helps a brother, they are like a walled city."

Yet, because God's call to each of us is so unique and intimately personal, we all realize the need at times to be alone, to get away from everyone else and from all their noises, so that we can truly hear ourselves and our God in the depths where we are one. This is something that it is sometimes difficult to find in our modern world, at least for any duration of time. Men set out on solitary camping trips or hiking to find it. Or find some hideouts deep within a city. But these men are exceptional. Cistercian life has always been intensely communal, giving the monks that strong support that a like-minded, closely-knit community can. The strict silence, the cloisters and gardens and corners of the church were meant to provide what solitude was needed.

One day in 1941 a young teacher from Saint Bonaventure's College stood on a dirt road in the valley below Gethsemani Abbey. As he looked up at the enclosure walls he asked himself, knowing his thirst for solitude: Could I ever live enclosed by those walls? Twenty-three years later he walked along that same dirt road and gently laughed at himself. As usual, he thought, I was looking in the wrong direction. As Thomas Merton, now Father M. Louis, stood there looking up at the abbey and its walls, to his back was the beginning of a dirt road that wound up what the monks called Mount Calvary. The road led to his little hermitage at the edge of the woods. Father Louis, though not alone in this, did much to re-open for the Cistercians the possibility to go apart from the community into a more solitary life.

Today not only has almost every Cistercian monastery some hermitages where the individual monk or nun can go apart for a day or a week or a month, but many also have one or more members who after years in community now live apart on a more permanent basis. The abbeys with their sizeable holdings provide the possible ambience for an individual to find a solitary spot that will not be encroached upon. Usually the cenobitic community will take care of many of the practical needs of the hermit, such as food supply, medical care, etc. The hermit does not live as a parasite. He makes his contribution to the community. It may be the very important one of serving as a spiritual father to many of the monks. He may also exercise some craft in his cell which brings in some income for them all or in some other way he may join in the work of the community. But most important he is there as a powerful reminder to the monks who might get too taken up with all the doings of the abbey that the Cistercian way is above all and before all a way that constantly seeks contemplative union with God in Christ. Everything else is geared to this one necessary thing.

Incorporation into the Cistercian Way

When men enter a monastery seeking to follow upon the Cistercian way, they may enter upon that way without delay. Unlike some other vocations, such as diocesan priesthood or missionary activity, where it is often necessary to undertake years of preparation and study before one can actually begin to carry out the vocation, the Cistercian from the day he enters the monastery walks in the Cistercian way. Undoubtedly as time goes on, through prayer and practice, through study and experience, he will enter more and more deeply into the way. But from the first day all is available to him. However, prudence and the law of the Church require that he only gradually and with due experience and discernment commit himself to this way and undertake all the obligations of full committed membership in the community.

Most Cistercian communities encourage a person interested in the life to make a number of shorter stays at the monastery. At the same time he is encouraged to visit other monasteries, to see alternate forms of Christian monastic life and to see also how the Cistercian life is lived in other monasteries. Each monastery has its own particular flavor. Many factors contribute to this: size, geographical location, leadership, house of origin or mother-house, make-up of the community, means of self-support, social and cultural environment. The daily experience of Cistercian life is quite different in a community where the fewness of numbers allows for and demands a primary relationship with everyone in the community. A monk can more easily get lost in a large community and also choose his primary friends. In a large community there is necessarily a lot more movement and activity. The liturgy will probably be done with a greater richness. The educational and cultural opportunities may be many more. The work program will have to be more fully developed to support the large numbers, offering a broader variety of work possibilities. And there will usually be a larger guesthouse program. A community in a poorer area will usually live more poorly and simply.

Some communities seem more oriented toward work or the penitential aspects of the life, while others are more contemplatively oriented and give those factors which most directly foster contemplation a higher priority. Beneath all the perceptible externals, though, there is a certain indefinable spirit that each community has. It is often this that the candidate gets in touch with and senses that this is his true home. He will see aspects that he likes better in other houses. He will find things in his chosen house that he could wish were different. Yet in sum, this particular monastery seems to be the place for him. Usually, visiting other monasteries only confirms this.

Of course, the vocation father will first have explored whether the candidate has sufficiently considered other ways of life: married life, single life in the world, diocesan priesthood, active religious life, other forms of monastic life. A reasonableness has to prevail here or the candidate could spend his whole life exploring. But a reasonable exploration is called for.

When a person seriously judges that this is the community to which he is called or he judges he needs a deeper and fuller experience of the life in this community to move toward such a judgment, he will usually be invited for what is being called an observership period: a month or two or three, lived within the community, usually taking full part in the novitiate program. With the successful completion of this, the candidate and the community come to a more definitive decision about the man's entrance into the Cistercian way. At this point the candidate will return home and take care of his responsibilities: perhaps resigning a job, selling a property or placing it in the hands of a trustee, investing his funds and handing over the administration of them to another, disposing of all his temporalities. He comes to the monastery for his novitiate a free man. Yet at the same time his temporalities are prudently arranged so that if he should decide to leave before his final commitment, they will be there to help him get a start again in the secular world. We usually do not encourage candidates to give away all they possess at this point. That comes later on.

Although it is no longer required by the common law of the Church, most Cistercian communities still give their candidates a preparatory period called postulancy before they begin their novitiate properly so called. This is usually not distinct from the novitiate program and varies in length from a month to a year. It gives the candidate a time in which to settle in and get used to things so that when he begins his novitiate he can freely concentrate on it.

In our Cistercian communities the novitiate is usually two years long. Only one year is required by the universal law of the Church. But the enclosed life is very special. It takes longer for the reality of its demands to seep deep into the spirit. All novelty has to wear off. The monotony has to take hold, a freeing monotony which the true contemplative welcomes. The excitement of new friends has to give way to the deeper relationship of brothers who are in it together all the way. The space opens for the divine romance to become central and begin to reveal some of its exigencies.

Two years will hardly begin to reveal them, but it will be enough to make consideration of a temporary commitment to this Cistercian way meaningful. It is only when we are in some way committed to the relationship, come what may, that it can begin to reveal something of its potential and of its demands. The years of temporary commitment, at least three and often more, are in many ways a prolongation of the novitiate, something introduced into monastic life by the Church only in this century. Often a candidate enters upon this with his mind and heart already very much set upon a lifetime commitment. Nonetheless, it is temporary and challenges him each day in preparation for the time when it will truly become "until death."

Cistercian monasteries do not have classes or groups who enter together and pass through the novitiate together and go on to vows together as is the case in some of the more active religious orders. Everything is done individually as an individual and very personal decision. It may happen that more than one candidate moves on together. I entered the same day as two others. We each made our first vows on different days. One of these men left rather than taking final vows in our community and is today superior in another monastic rite. Four of us were consecrated monks together, largely for practical reasons. I was off helping to start a new monastery when my three years of temporary profession were complete. More decisive in choosing the date was our desire to celebrate the day with greater solemnity and yet not overburden the community.

A careful discernment of the working of God within the temporary professed, a discernment which involves the whole community to some extent but most especially the man himself and his abbot, determines the time for moving ahead to the final commitment and consecration as a monk. The abbot consulted only his council when he admitted the candidate to the novitiate. When the novice sought to make first profession, the whole community of monks had to vote on his acceptance. With their approval the abbot made the decision. When it comes to the final step the abbot again seeks the consent of the community to move ahead, but it is he standing before God who makes the decision, gives the call and consecrates his son to God.

With these lifetime vows, which for the Cistercian are solemn vows, and consecration as a monk during the holy Sacrifice of the Mass, we are made monks, men belonging wholly to the Lord. As Blessed Benedict says in his Rule, not even our bodies are any longer our own. We can no longer contract marriage, for we are given wholly to Another forever. We can no longer possess anything as our own. Given to God we in a sense belong to the monastery as does everything we use or have with the permission of the abbot. These radical human rights are given back to the Lord; the right to give ourselves in marriage, our right to possess. Before the day of our solemn profession, we give away all we possess and assign all our inheritance to others. Now is the time to fulfill the evangelical counsel: "God, sell what you have and give to the poor and come follow me." There is to be no looking back. We will expect to receive all that we need from the father of the monastery. This is one way in which we begin to respond to the Lord's precept to become as little children and enjoy something of the freedom of the sons of God.

Sometime after solemn profession some monks will be called by the abbot to go on to the diaconate or priesthood. The abbot will listen carefully to what the Lord is saying within his son. He will consult the community. There will be the usual course of studies, prolonged so as to fit gracefully into the Cistercian way. The man remains always first of all a monk. Our communities like any other Catholic community need the ministry of priests to lead us in Eucharist, to absolve our sins, to bring us the Lord's anointing in our hour of sickness. Our guests, too, will look to us for sacramental ministry. So God calls some monks to ministerial priesthood. Outside the times of actual ministry, though, the priest will be indistinguishable from all his fellow monks, exercising in the Work of God and all the other practices of our common life our common baptismal priesthood.

Through the years canonists and theologians have debated whether a monk can ever be dispensed of his solemn vows and return to the lay state, leaving behind in some way his consecration as a monk. Those who argue in the affirmative have on their side the apparent practice of the Church. Christ's Vicar in Christ's name can release one from the vows made to Christ our God. Others would argue that in fact one never ceases to be a monk. A consecration is irrevocable. The Church in Christ's name recognizes the person's need, whether through weakness or because Christ in some mysterious way is calling the man on to some other vocation, to be released from the observance of the consequences of his vows. We will probably have to wait until we see all things in heaven to know what indeed is the fact of the matter. In any case the dispensation of a monk from his solemn vows certainly should be something that is most exceptional. At the same time there is no room here for any judgments. When we consider the magnificent things God has accomplished through some men who have been dispensed from their vows, there seems little doubt, using Jesus' standard of judging a tree by its fruit, that he himself has been at work in the new vocations he has given his sons.

9

At the Heart of the Church
and the World

The Cistercian is indeed a marginal person. With the exception of few very extraordinary persons who are extraordinarily connected, like the late Thomas Merton, we have actually very little understanding of what is going on in the world as history draws toward a close and ideologies melt into a worldwide consumer society where a privileged few rapidly consume the resources God so lavishly afforded the human family and the rest of that family is consumed in their service or by the lacks that the privileged have produced. The headlines do penetrate the enclosure. Some monks devote more time to the media but garner little more real knowledge than the average busy citizen. Economic and political forces play out their game while the monk for the most part goes quietly about his daily round of liturgy, *lectio*, and labor.

Are we monastics really that irrelevant?

I hope not. I believe not. In fact, I believe enough in the relevance of the Cistercian to the course of salvation history to literally stake my life on it.

We are marginal. But there are two margins. An outer margin and an inner margin. We are I believe at the inner margin, at the heart of the world, one with Christ, the source of all its being and life.

Creation is not a finished product cast out by God at some moment and left to go its own course. Rather at every moment creation comes forth from the creating Word of God. And that God of love, who so loves his creation, in his love has given it over to the service and stewardship of the summit of his creation, his beloved sons and daughters, we humans who have been called to be uniquely one with his Son. In that love he has decided that the way that he will bring his creation forth tomorrow and the next day will depend in part on our prayer and lack of it. Here is one place where the Cistercian's life is very relevant. For he is called to pray night and day for the good of the people. Our prayer of intercession is powerful because it is a response to the powerful promise of our God and is called forth and energized by his all-powerful grace.

But our prayer is effective not only when it is one of intercession. All our prayer is intercessory. For God does not regard our lips. He looks to our hearts. It is our heartfelt concerns he attends to every time we come to him in prayer whether or not we express those concerns at that moment or even advert to them. He sees the cares of our hearts and he has care. This is why it is important that we Cistercians do keep in some contact with the needs of the people, whether it be through the news media or by more personal correspondence. We need to remain sensitively aware of the anguish of our sisters and brothers and carry this compassionately in our hearts. It would never be enough if we frequently made prayers of intercession, as we do, especially when we are gathered together in Eucharist or office. Our whole lives, in their caring love, must be intercession.

Our explicit prayer is more frequently a prayer of praise and thanksgiving as we offer Eucharist (*eucharistia*) and make our own the words of the psalmist. These great prayers of thanksgiving readily flow from the depths of our being as the Holy Spirit through the activity of her gifts makes us ever more aware of the bounty of our God in all his creation and of his wonder and beauty and divinity beyond it all. Holy, holy, holy is our God.

But the Cistercians' favorite prayer is that of contemplation, the prayer of being. In this prayer we offer God not just our thoughts or our words or our sentiments and aspirations. We offer him our very selves. And who are we? We are the Christ, made intimately one with him, the Son, through the mysterious operation of baptism. We are the Son to the Father in the Holy Spirit. It is in this prayer of being that we not only offer to the Father a praise and thanksgiving that is worthy of him but we are lifted up into him, into the very heart of the Trinity. And in being so lifted up, because of our intimate bonding with every other member of Christ and with every other member of our human race, all are lifted up into a more life-giving union with God.

The Cistercian may not be too cognizant of all that is going on on the outer surface of humanity's activities nor even of some of the deeper things. He may, like the heart, not even sense explicitly many of the more superficial wounds of the body. But like the heart his constant quiet repetition of his daily duty is what sends healing elements to those wounded areas. He is called to serve the whole body, without ceasing, in a truly life-giving ministry. Only a knowledgeable and attentive ear can know the significance of the quiet throb that can scarcely be detected much of the time. When the heart is quietly fulfilling its role, we can easily enough forget about it but we certainly cannot live without it.

Why this waste? If the monk is not living a life of constant prayer or at least striving towards that then his life is a waste and a scandal. Let the monastery be sold and the money given to the poor. But if he is indeed living such a life, then he is doing a good thing and it will not be taken away from him. Wherever Christ's Gospel is proclaimed this will be found.

The Cistercian lives at the heart of the Church and world not only for others but to invite others to come themselves to a deep heart, to come to the center of their own being, to the Source of all, and be each themselves a channel of that life into the world. The monastery stands apart, a sign that beckons. But it is not just a sign, as important as that is. It is in fact a place apart where all who hear the welcome can come, where they can find the quiet they need and the help they perhaps need to come to their own heart to find the peace and joy that is rightfully theirs as the beloved of God and to be enabled to bring that peace and joy back into the frenetic activities of our redeemed world.

We believe in the power of intercessory prayer. We believe in the transformation of human consciousness through contemplation. We believe in the solidarity of the Body of Christ and of the whole human family. For these reasons we believe in the revelance of our marginality. We believe that to live at the heart of the Church and the world is the most significant way in which we, in accord with our God-given vocation to be Cistercians, can best live our lives.

We believe in the Cistercian way. And even though we but stumble along it, we are grateful for the divine call to walk in this way.

Appendices

The Four Evangelists of Cîteaux

Four of the early Cistercian Fathers, because of the depth and beauty of the writings in which they have set forth their understanding of the inner spirit that animated the Cistercian reform, have traditionally been referred to as the Evangelists of Cîteaux: Bernard of Clairvaux, William of Saint Thierry, Guerric of Igny, and Aelred of Rievaulx. These men shared deeply in the charism of the founders of the order and were undoubtedly inspired in the way in which they wrote of it. To them before all others Cistercians and others through the centuries have looked in their quest to understand the Cistercian spirit and, according to their vocation, to live it.

Bernard of Clairvaux

Bernard of Fontaines (born 1090) was by origin a man of the upper class. His family had its place among the nobility of the emerging French nation. He was well educated. His writings give evidence of some familiarity with the classics and an excellent training in composition. He uses every literary form, is masterfully at home in all of them. In the fullest sense of the word, he is literate.

Bernard had extraordinary powers of leadership. When he decided Cîteaux was the right answer, he did not go alone. He led thirty relatives and friends into the marshes. He was not a naive lad, unfamiliar with the ways of the world. He pursued a married brother into a front-line army camp and into a prison. He spoke frankly to uncles and brothers and friends alike. He would be well prepared and knowledgeable when he later offered advice and direction to kings and princes, bishops and clerics, knights and scholars. And he could identify with the poor.

The man who wrote *The Steps of Humility* was not humble by origin, nature or temperament. It was a virtue—he knew from experience—that had to be cultivated at a price. The aspirant of twenty-two years must also have been mature spiritually. Otherwise it would hardly have been possible for him to have reached so rapidly that spiritual fullness which would have allowed the abbot of Cîteaux, Saint Stephen Harding, to send him forth as the spiritual father of Cîteaux's third daughter house, Clairvaux. He had known the rigor of a Cistercian novitiate—made more rigorous by his own zeal— and a couple of years of community life as a simple monk. He was ready for the years of ever more weighty responsibility as the abbot of a rapidly growing community. Early on he was plagued by serious ill health and used the opportunity to compose his first published work, a four-sermon commentary on the *Missus est*, the Gospel account of the annunciation and incarnation. From his earliest days as abbot he had to travel much—much for an ordinary Cistercian abbot, though not much in comparison with what the future would demand of him—seeing bishops and nobles to get the permissions, backing and finances for Clairvaux's initial foundations—the first in what would be a steadily growing stream. His life was enriched by sharing it with some wonderful friends: William of Champeaux, his bishop; William of Saint Thierry, his closest friend who convalesced with him; Guerric of Igny, who came to Clairvaux in 1123, a saintly scholar with years of learning and prayerful solitude behind him; and Bernard's own remarkable brothers and uncles.

The Steps of Humility with their rich irony won him ever greater fame. He was called upon to defend the Cistercian reform in his *Apologia* and to speak out on theological questions, *On Grace and Free Will* and *Against Abelard*. He was sought as a mediator and advocate, especially in the healing of the papal schism (1130–1138). For this he traveled widely, always attracting large numbers and bringing many back to Clairvaux. In 1136 he began a series of sermons commenting on the *Song of Songs*, a labor he continued until his death in 1153. It is to this tremendously rich collection we look before all else for his spiritual legacy. Before he died he saw one of the monks he sent forth to Italy as a founding abbot, Bernard Pignatelli, elevated to the papal throne as Pope Eugene III, and for him Bernard wrote his *Five Books on Consideration*. Because of his obedient preaching of what proved to be a disastrous crusade, Bernard's life ended somewhat under a cloud but his evident holiness could not be denied and he was canonized twenty-one years after his death.

William of Saint Thierry

William had been a good scholarly Black Benedictine for some years, a highly respected monk, probably prior of his monastery, when in company with his abbot he visited Bernard of Clairvaux in 1119. The visit had a profound impact on him. Thirty years later he would still write of it in awed terms, using an exalted liturgical analogy. It was an hour of conversion for him. He wanted to become what young Bernard was. At almost that same hour he himself was chosen to be an abbot. And so he had a community with whom to share his new quest. Many of his treatises are edited from conferences he gave his communities.

First William explored what contemplation is and how one can hope to acquire it. This is his treatise *On Contemplating God*. The way is love and so he turns his consideration to love: *On the Nature and Dignity of Love*. Then, in the true Cistercian way, he knew he had to get to know the lover and the power at work in him—grace.

Like so many of the other Cistercian Fathers, he then produced his treatise on man: *On the Nature of Body and Soul*. His treatise on grace, which followed, took the form of a *Commentary on the Epistle to the Romans*, which is largely drawn from Saint Augustine. William relied very heavily on the Fathers of the Church and did not hesitate to use their very texts and words. Now that he was ready to turn his attention to the text that was at the heart of all Cistercian mystical doctrine, the *Song of Songs*, he did not immediately launch out on his own. He had begun an explanation of it with Bernard which he published as the *Brevis Commentatio* (the *Brief Commentary*). Next he searched through all of Ambrose of Milan and Gregory the Great and drew out all they had to say, verse by verse, on the great love song. With all this behind him, he was ready to begin his own commentary, his *Exposition on the Song of Songs*.

Rich additional light is thrown upon this whole development by William's very personal *Meditations*, which were written through these same years and finally published "to help young men to learn how to pray," after he had resigned as abbot in 1135 and entered the Cistercian Abbey of Signy. We have from the same period a letter, or rather a treatise on the Eucharist, a response to a request which indicates as do many other incidental writings, how important a place the Eucharist held in the lives of the Cistercian Fathers.

As one grows in union with Christ, one comes to have his mind and heart, to share all his loves and concerns. The Fathers were men of the Church. As much as they longed for Mary's part, for Rachel's embraces, they accepted Martha's role when such was demanded and became fruitful like Lia. When Abelard imperiled the true faith and true theology, William forsook his holy leisure and his love song and spoke out on the true nature of faith and its content—*The Mirror of Faith* and *The Enigma of Faith*—for the sake of the young monks in his community and all who were being influenced and confused by the subtle dialectic of that cocky genius. After the battle was over, William sought deeper solitude for a time with the nearby Carthusians. To express his fraternal gratitude to them and again to help the young, he wrote his magnificent synthesis, *The Golden Epistle*. Finally, as life drew to a close he began to paint an idealized icon of all his spiritual teaching in the biography of his idol and lifelong inspiration, the incarnation of all he strove for, his beloved friend, the abbot of Clairvaux.

While we do not know the date of William's birth, we do know that he died on the birthday of Our Lady, September 8, 1148.

Guerric of Igny

In some respects Guerric of Igny is truly in the middle of things. He is the favored disciple of Bernard of Clairvaux. Later, Guerric had Bernard as his Father Immediate,[22] while at the same time he himself was the Father Immediate of William of Saint Thierry who had become a monk of Signy. Guerric entered Clairvaux probably around 1123, before Bernard had as yet been catapulted into his worldwide role and still was able to spend considerable time at home with his community. Bernard took special interest in the men in formation, and there is good reason to believe that Guerric in a very

[22]"Father Immediate" is the title given by the monks of an abbey to the abbot of the monastery which originally sent monks to start the abbey. This abbot retained a certain paternal responsibility for the community and was required to visit them at least once a year (now usually every three years). In the course of his visit, he hears what each monk has to say about the well being of the community and its particular needs. He then gives a report of his findings (the visitation card) to the community and also makes a report to the General Chapter.

particular way claimed his attention. The choice of Guerric as abbot of Igny undoubtedly came about in part through the influence of Bernard, which would indicate that the abbot of Clairvaux saw in him a man who had grasped well the spirituality he sought to impart and who would be able to pass it on to others. For his part, Guerric, on his regular visits to his daughter house Signy, because of his love for his master, would have sought out his master's closest friend and would have tried to learn from William all he could about their beloved Bernard. It was perhaps William's Father Immediate, just as it was Aelred's, who encouraged him to edit some of his past jottings and also to put on paper his later works.

We have only fifty-three liturgical sermons and one sermon from Guerric's commentary on the *Song of Songs*. Their simplicity, clarity, and practicality make these sermons particularly attractive. They are, perhaps, among the least edited of the writings that have come down to us from our Fathers, the closest to what the monks might have actually heard as they sat in chapter. Guerric's sermons are full of good, down-to-earth, practical teaching. There is a complete though concise theology of work, of poverty, of silence, etc. And yet his doctrine is not pedestrian. It is truly Cistercian—the ideal of contemplative union with God is always present. Guerric makes no bones about it—all are called to this union and many of his monks are happily experiencing it.

Aelred of Rievaulx

Although not the best known of the Cistercian Fathers, Aelred of Rievaulx with his true humanness is one of the most loved. In these days when our common concern is turned towards the renewal of Cistercian life in all its aspects and when there is such emphasis placed upon the full development of human potentialities and values, the frank and not untraditional statement of monastic values by a true Christian humanist has a bracing effect. This gifted, sensitive monk entered the Cistercian order while the last of the original founders were probably still alive. He knew personally and perhaps intimately the great theologian of the Cistercian spirit, Bernard of Clairvaux. As Aelred's Father Immediate Bernard asked Aelred to write *The Mirror of Charity*, Aelred's most basic and important work. His more famous treatise, *Spiritual Friendship*, cannot be properly understood if it is not seen in the context of *The Mirror*.

Aelred was still quite young—only 32—and young in the order—seven years professed—when he was sent on an important mission to Rome in 1142. The controversy over the bishopric of York greatly interested Bernard of Clairvaux, so this reason, as well as the fact that Bernard was the Father Immediate of Rievaulx, made it fitting that the emissary stop at Clairvaux both on his way to Rome and on his return. These were probably the first meetings Bernard had with the exceptional young monk, who was gifted with a rich and varied background. Aelred, the son of a priest, had been raised for the most part in the court of the King of Scotland. To Bernard who had been abbot since he was twenty-five, after only two years of professed life, Aelred did not appear so young and certainly not inexperienced. The former courtier was ready to serve as novice master of a rapidly growing abbey—founded but ten years earlier, it already housed some three hundred monks and lay brothers—and soon thereafter to be sent to head one of Rievaulx's early foundations. What Bernard did see in the young monk was that he had a thorough and clear grasp of the basic teaching of the School of Love. And so, employing his authority to overcome an understandable diffidence, Bernard required of the young novice master an authoritative manual for the novices of the order.

Aelred enjoyed writing and produced a number of historical treatises as well as some spiritual ones written for his sister and some friends. One of his most beautiful pieces is his own *Pastoral Prayer*. Every abbot, indeed everyone called to pastoral ministry could well make this prayer his own. Aelred suffered very much from ill health but did not find as much leisure for writing as one might have expected for he allowed his infirmary cell to be constantly invaded by his beloved sons. Nonetheless, on his death bed he completed his treatise *On the Soul* before rendering his own soul to Jesus Love in 1167.

These four fathers have left us a tremendous corpus of writings which reveal in its fullest the way of the Cistercians. Young Cistercian monks and nuns spend much of their early years in the monastery studying these fathers or rather allowing these fathers to draw them ever more deeply into the way of the Cistercians, a ministry which these monks who are so fully alive now in the Lord and can be so present to us through their writings continue to offer us all the days of our lives as we continue to walk in this way.

The Little Exordium

*The Little Exordium takes the form of a letter composed by the
founders of Cîteaux or the New Monastery. It was probably composed gradually through a number of years, being completed just
prior to the papal approval of the first Charter of Charity in 1119.
It seeks to establish the legitimacy of the establishment of the New
Monastery which developed into a new monastic order.*

Letter of the First Cistercians
to All Their Successors

We Cistercians, the original founders of this monastery, make
known to our successors through this present writing how canonically, by what authority, and by which persons, as well as at what
period of time, their monastery and manner of living had its beginning. We publish the sincere truth of this matter that they may the
more tenaciously love the place as well as the observance of the holy
Rule therein, which we ourselves with the grace of God have only
just begun; that they may pray for us who have sustained inde-
fatigably the burden and the heat of the day; and that they may labor
unto death on the strait and narrow way prescribed by the Rule, so
that after they have put down the burden of the flesh they may re-
pose happily in eternal rest. Amen.

I. The Beginning of the Monastery of Cîteaux

In the year 1098 of the Incarnation of our Lord, Robert of blessed
memory, the first abbot of the monastery of Molesme which was
founded in the diocese of Langres, and certain brethren of the same
monastery appeared before the venerable Hugh, then legate of the
Apostolic See and archbishop of the church of Lyons, and promised

to place their lives under the custody of the holy Rule of Father Benedict. For the unhindered realization of this intention, therefore, they begged him insistently to lend them the strength of his own support and of his apostolic authority. The legate, joyfully espousing their wish, laid down the foundations of their beginning with the following letter.

II. Letter of the Legate Hugh

Hugh, Archbishop of Lyons and legate of the Apostolic See to Robert, Abbot of Molesme, and to the brethren who together with him desire to serve God according to the Rule of Saint Benedict. Let it be known to all who rejoice in the progress of Holy Mother Church that you and certain of your sons, brothers of the monastery of Molesme, have stood in Our presence at Lyons and stated your wish to adhere henceforth more strictly and more perfectly to the Rule of blessed Benedict, which so far you have observed poorly and neglectfully in that monastery. But, since it is obvious that in view of many obstacles this could not be accomplished in the aforementioned place, We, providing for the welfare of both parties, those departing and those remaining, have concluded that it will be expedient for you to retire to another place which the Divine Munificence will point out to you, and there serve the Lord in a more salutary and peaceful manner. To you, therefore, who had at that time presented yourselves—Abbot Robert and brothers Alberic, Odo, John, Stephen, Letald, and Peter—as well as to all others whom you shall decide to add to your company according to the Rule and by common consultation, after deliberation We gave the order that you persevere in this holy endeavor. We confirm it forever by the authority of the Apostolic See through the impression of Our seal.

III. Departure of the Cistercian Monks from Molesme and Their Arrival at Cîteaux and the Monastery They Founded There

Afterwards, with the support of such great authority, the aforementioned abbot and his monks returned to Molesme and from that religious community selected like-minded associates who were devoted to the Rule, so that those who had spoken before the legate in Lyons and those who were selected from the community numbered twenty-one monks. Knit together in such a band, they eagerly set out for the solitude which was called Cîteaux. This place, situated in the diocese of Chalon, was inhabited only by wild beasts, since it was at that time unusual for men to enter there because of the density of the woods and thorny thickets. Arriving at this place the men of God found it all the more suitable for the religious life which they had already formulated in their minds and for which they had come here, the more despicable and inaccessible they realized it to be for seculars. After they had cut down and removed the dense woods and the thorny thickets, they began to construct a monastery there with the approval of the bishop of Chalon and with the consent of the territorial lord. For, inspired by the grace of God, these men, while still living in Molesme, often spoke to each other, lamented, and were saddened by the transgression of the Rule of Saint Benedict, the Father of Monks. They realized that they themselves and the other monks had promised by a solemn vow to observe this Rule, yet they had by no means kept it; and therefore they had knowingly committed the sin of perjury. For this reason they came into this solitude with the authority of the legate of the Apostolic See, as we mentioned, to fulfill their vows through the keeping of the holy Rule. Then, pleased with their holy fervor and having been requested in a letter by the aforementioned legate of the holy Roman Church, Lord Odo, the duke of Burgundy, with his means completed the wooden monastery which they had begun and provided them there for a long time with every necessity and generously supported them with land as well as livestock.

IV. How That Place Rose to an Abbey

At the same time, the abbot who had come here, upon the command of the aforementioned legate, received from the bishop of the diocese the shepherd's staff and the care of the monks; he also caused the brethren who had come with him to undertake their stability in that place in accordance with the Rule. This is how that monastery rose to an abbey canonically and with apostolic authority.

V. How Those from Molesme Harried the Pope in the Matter of Abbot Robert's Return

Shortly afterwards, some monks of Molesme, charged by their abbot, Lord Godfrey, who succeeded Robert, went to Rome to the lord Pope Urban. They demanded that the often mentioned Robert be restored to his former place. Moved by their importuning, the Pope ordered his legate, the venerable Hugh, to see to it that, if it could be done, the abbot should return and the monks who loved the solitude be left in peace.

VI. Letter of the Pope Regarding the Return of the Abbot

Bishop Urban, Servant of the Servants of God, to his venerable brother and fellow bishop Hugh, vicar of the Apostolic See: greeting and apostolic blessing. We have heard in council the great outcry of the brethren of Molesme who vehemently demanded the return of their abbot. Indeed, they have said that on account of that abbot's absence regular life in their monastery had been subverted and that they had become hateful to their lords and neighbors. Now at length, having been prevailed upon by Our brethren, We command Your Grace, by indicating that it would please Us, to see to it that, if it can be done, the abbot be restored from the solitude to the monastery. But if you cannot accomplish this, let it be your concern that those who love the solitude may live in peace and those who are in the monastery observe the regular discipline.

After the legate had read this apostolic letter, he summoned a number of men of authority and piety and decided the following about the matter.

VII. The Legate's Decision in the Whole Matter
Concerning the Monks of Molesme and Cîteaux

Hugh, Servant of the church of Lyons, to his most beloved brother Robert, bishop of Langres: greeting. We have considered it necessary to let Your Fraternity know what we have decided in the meeting recently held at Port-d'Anselle regarding the matter of the monastery of Molesme. Several monks from Molesme appeared before Us in that place with Your letter; they described to us the desolation and the ruin of their place, which the removal of the abbot Robert had brought upon them, and forcefully implored that he be given back to them as father. For, they had no hope that peace and quiet could return to the monastery of Molesme or that the full vigor of the monastic discipline could be restored to its pristine state in any other way. Present before us was also Brother Godfrey, whom You have installed as abbot of that monastery, who stated that he would gladly yield his place to the same Robert as his father if We should decide to send him back to the community of Molesme. After having considered Your request and that of the monks of Molesme and having reread the letter of the lord Pope addressed to Us in this matter, which entrusted the whole matter to Our disposition and judgment, We, upon the advice of many religious men, bishops as well as others, who were with Us in council, have at length decided to acquiesce in Your wish and theirs and return Robert to the monastery of Molesme. This shall be done in such a way that, before his return, he shall go to Chalon and surrender the staff and the care of the abbey into the hands of Our brother the bishop of Chalon, to whom he had sworn obedience as abbots customarily do. Also, he shall free and absolve the monks of the New Monastery, who made their profession and obedience to him as their abbot, from that profession and obedience. Thereupon he shall be released by that bishop from the profession of obedience he has made to him and to the diocese of Chalon.

We have also given permission to return with him to Molesme to all those brethren of the New Monastery who will follow him when he leaves it, provided that henceforth neither side will attempt to lure or receive anyone to its side, except in the manner which blessed Benedict prescribed for the admission of monks of a known monastery. After he has done all this, We release him to Your Grace, so that You may restore him as the abbot of Molesme; in such a way, however, that, if with his usual inconstancy he should again leave that same monastery, no one shall be put in his place during the lifetime of the above named abbot Godfrey, without Our and Your, as well as Godfrey's assent. We ordain by apostolic authority that all these provisions have the force of law.

With regard to the aforementioned abbot Robert's chapel [instruments] and the other things which he took with him upon his departure from the monastery of Molesme and with which he went to the bishop of Chalon and to the New Monastery, We have ordered that everything shall remain unharmed with the brethren of the New Monastery, with the exception of a certain breviary which they may keep with the approval of the monks of Molesme, until the feast of Saint John the Baptist, so that they may copy it.

Present at this decision were the bishops Norgaud of Autun, Walter of Chalon, Beraud [Herardus] of Mâcon, Pons of Belley and the abbots Peter of Tournus, Jarente of Dijon, Gaucerand of Ainay, as well as Peter, chamberlain of the lord Pope, and many other honorable men of good character.

That abbot approved and executed all this, releasing the Cistercians from the obedience which they had promised him either at that place or in Molesme. Likewise, the lord bishop Walter of Chalon released the abbot from the care of that monastery. And so he returned with a few monks who did not find the solitude to their liking.

This is how through apostolic favor the two abbeys remained in peace and complete freedom. As a shield for his defense the returning abbot took along the following letter to his bishop.

VIII. Commendation of Abbot Robert

Walter, servant of the church of Chalon, to His most beloved brother and fellow-bishop Robert, bishop of Langres: greeting. Be it known to You that according to the decision of the lord archbishop Hugh, We have released brother Robert, to whom We had entrusted that abbey in Our diocese which is called New Monastery, from the solemn profession made to the diocese of Chalon as well as from the obedience he promised to Us. He himself as well has released and freed those monks who have decided to remain in the aforesaid New Monastery from the obedience and the profession they had vowed to him. I enjoin you, therefore, not to fear to accept him and to treat him as a man in good standing.

IX. About the Election of Alberic, the First Abbot of the Monastery of Cîteaux

Deprived of its shepherd, the community of Cîteaux assembled and through a regular election elevated a certain brother by the name of Alberic to be its abbot. He was well versed in both divine and human letters, and a lover of the Rule and the brethren. For a long time he had held the office of prior in the monastery of Molesme as well as here, and he had labored much and long for the brethren to move from Molesme to this place, for which endeavor he had had to suffer many insults, prison and beatings.

X. About the Roman Privilege

After much resistance the aforementioned Alberic accepted the pastoral care. As a man of admirable forethought, he began to weigh what storms of tribulations might at one time or another shake and disturb the house entrusted to his care. Taking precaution for the future, with the consent of the brethren he sent two monks, John and Ilbodus, to Rome. Through them he petitioned the lord Pope Paschal that, under the wings of apostolic protection, his monastery might forever remain peaceful and safe from the pressure of any ecclesiastical or lay person. The two brethren just named, supported by the sealed letters of the aforementioned archbishop Hugh, of John and Benedict, cardinals of the Roman church, as well as of bishop Walter of Chalon, went safely to Rome and returned before Pope Paschal had faltered in the captivity of the emperor. They brought back his apostolic privilege composed entirely according to the wishes of the abbot and his associates. We have thought it appropriate to hand down these letters as well as the Roman privilege in this little work, so that our successors might realize with how much deliberation and authority their monastery has been founded.

XI. Letter of the Cardinals John and Benedict

To our lord and father, Pope Paschal, to whom always and everywhere the greatest praise is due, John and Benedict, with total submission. Since it is Your office to provide for the needs of all churches and to give a helping hand to the just wishes of petitioners, and since the Christian religion must grow by leaning on the support of Your justice, we beg Your Holiness most insistently to lend a merciful hearing to the carriers of this letter who, upon our advice, have been sent to Your Paternity by certain religious brethren. In truth, they ask that the decree which they received from Your predecessor, our lord Pope Urban of blessed memory, in regard to the peace and stability of their monastic life and which, in accordance with the same decree, the archbishop of Lyons, then legate, and some of his fellow bishops and abbots, had established between them and the abbey of Molesme, from which they had seceded in consideration of the religious life, may through the privilege of your authority forever remain undisturbed. Indeed, we ourselves have seen and vouch for the evidence of their truly religious life.

XII. Letter of Hugh of Lyons

To his most reverend father and lord, Pope Paschal, Hugh, servant of the church of Lyons, with total submission. The brethren bearing the present letter, journeying to the Highness of Your Paternity have passed through Our lands. Since they live in Our province, namely in the diocese of Chalon, they asked Our unworthy self for a letter of recommendation to Your Highness. You should know, then, that they come from a place which is called New Monastery. They migrated to that place, after seceding from the community of Molesme with their abbot, in order to lead a stricter and more consecrated life according to the Rule of blessed Benedict which they had resolved to keep by abandoning the usages of certain monasteries maintaining that in their weakness they were unfit to bear such a great burden. For that reason the brethren of Molesme and certain other monks of the neighborhood do not cease to attack and disturb them, thinking that in the eyes of the world they themselves are valued less and looked upon with contempt, if such exceptional and new kinds of monks are seen living in their midst. Therefore, We humbly and trustfully ask You, Beloved Father, that You receive with Your usual kindness these brothers who, after the Lord, place all their trust in You and therefore seek refuge in Your apostolic authority; also, that You free them and their place from such molestation and disturbance, and corroborate this through a privilege of Your authority. For they are the poor of Christ: they have no defense through riches or power against their enemies, but place all their hope in God's mercy and Yours.

XIII.   *Letter of the Bishop of Chalon*

To his venerable Father, Pope Paschal, Walter, bishop of Chalon: greetings and due submission. As Your Holiness ardently desires the advancement of the faithful in the true religion, so must they not lack the shelter of Your protection and the encouragement of Your consolation. We therefore humbly beg that You approve what has been done in accordance with Your predecessor's order and the decision and the rescript of the Archbishop of Lyons, then legate of the Apostolic See, as well as other bishops and abbots who had been witnesses and participants in this decision, with regard to certain brethren. Longing for a stricter life they have, upon the advice of saintly men, departed from the monastery of Molesme; Divine Mercy has placed them in Our diocese; their envoys, the bearers of this letter stand before You. We also beg You to deign to corroborate with a privilege of Your authority that that place might remain a free abbey in perpetuity, saving, however, the canonical reverence due Our person and Our successors. The abbot whom We have installed in that place and the other brethren also ask Your Kindness most insistently for this confirmation to secure their peace.

XIV. *The Roman Privilege*

Bishop Paschal, Servant of the Servants of God, to the venerable Alberic, abbot of New Monastery, situated in the episcopate of Chalon, and to all his legitimate successors in perpetuity. An aspiration which is obviously aimed at a religious purpose and the welfare of souls is to be fulfilled by the will of God without delay. Therefore, sons most beloved in the Lord, We accede to Your petition without any difficulty, because we applaud Your religious fervor with paternal affection. We decree, therefore, that the place which You have chosen in order to live in monastic tranquillity, shall be secure and free from the annoyance of all men; also, that the abbey shall exist there forever and be particularly sheltered under the protection of the Apostolic See, saving the canonical reverence due to the diocese of Chalon. By the words of this present decree We, therefore, forbid anyone whomsoever to change Your way of life or to receive monks of Your monastery, which is called New Monastery, without the recommendation demanded by the Rule, or to disturb Your community through any kind of guile or violence. The settlement of the controversy between You and the monastery of Molesme—which Our brother, the bishop of Lyons, then vicar of the Apostolic See, made together with the bishops of his province and other religious men, at the command of Our predecessor, Urban the Second of apostolic memory—We confirm as eminently reasonable. You, sons most beloved and most dear in Christ, must, therefore, remember that one part of You has left the broad roads of the world; yet another part, the paths not strait enough of a monastery too relaxed. In order that You may be considered more and more deserving of this grace, You must work to keep always in Your hearts the fear and love of God so that to the degree that you are free from the noises and pleasures of the world, by so much the more You should strive to please God with all the powers of Your mind and soul. Indeed, should any archbishop or bishop, emperor or king, prince or duke, count or viscount, judge or any other clerical or lay person whosoever knowingly dare to counteract this Our constitution, and upon two or three warnings not make amends for his wrongdoing through an adequate satisfaction, let him be deprived of the powers and honor of his dignity and let him know that he is liable to divine judgment because of the wrong he has done; and let him be excluded from the most holy Body and Blood of our God and our Lord, Jesus Christ, and undergo severe vengeance at the Last Judgment. May the peace of our Lord Jesus Christ rest upon all those who respect the rights of this monastery so that they may receive the fruit of their good deed here on the earth and find the reward of eternal peace before the stern Judge.

XV. The Institutes of the Cistercian Monks Who Departed from Molesme

Thereupon the abbot and his brethren, mindful of their vows, unanimously resolved to establish and to keep the Rule of blessed Benedict in that place. They rejected what was contrary to the Rule, namely full mantles and furs, as well as shirts of fine linen, cowls and breeches, combs and blankets, mattresses, a wide variety of dishes in the refectory as well as fat and everything else which was against the purity of the Rule. Making thus the rectitude of the Rule the foremost concern of their life, they followed or conformed to the pathway of the Rule in ecclesiastical as well as in other observances. In this way, having put off the old man, they rejoiced in putting on the new.

And since they could not find either in the Rule or in the life of Saint Benedict that this teacher had possessed churches or altars, offerings or burial dues, tithes of other people, or ovens or mills or manors or serfs, and that women had ever entered his monastery or been buried there, with the exception of his sister, they renounced all these things saying: Where the blessed Father Benedict teaches that the monk must avoid worldly affairs, there he distinctly explains that these things must not have any place in the actions or in the hearts of monks who must live up to the etymology of their name by fleeing all these things. They also said that the holy Fathers, who were the instruments of the Holy Spirit and whose decisions it is a sacrilege to transgress, divided tithes into four distinct parts: namely, one part for the bishop; the second for the parish priest; the third for guests who come to the church, or else for widows and orphans or for the poor who have nothing else to live on; the fourth for the repair of churches. And since in this list they did not find mention of the monk who possesses his own lands whence he gains his livelihood by his own labor and by keeping animals, they rejected this as an unjust usurpation of the rights of others. Thus having rejected the riches of this world, the new soldiers of Christ, poor with the poor Christ, began to consult with one another as to the question of the way by which, and with what work or occupation, they should provide in this life for themselves as well as for guests who would come, rich and poor alike, whom according to the Rule they should receive as Christ.

Thereupon they decided to admit, with the permission of their bishop, bearded lay-brothers and to treat them in life and death as their equals, excepting only the status as monks; and to admit also hired workers. For they realized that without the help of these men they would be unable to observe fully the precepts of the Rule by day and by night. They also decided to accept landed properties which lay removed from the dwellings of men, as well as vineyards and meadows and woods and also streams, in order to install mills— but only for their own use—and for fishing, and horses and various cattle useful to the requirements of men. And while they established granges for the practice of agriculture in a number of places, they decreed that the aforementioned lay-brothers, and not the monks, should manage those houses, because according to the Rule the dwelling place of monks ought to be within their cloister. Since those holy men knew that blessed Benedict had built his monasteries not in towns or around fortified places or in villages, but in places removed from the traffic of men, they promised to imitate him. And since he placed twelve monks and a father abbot in new monasteries, they decided to proceed in the same manner.

XVI. About Their Sorrow

It caused some sorrow to the aforementioned abbot and man of God and to those with him that in those days only seldom did anyone come there in order to follow after them. For the holy men longed to hand down to their successors for the future benefit of many this treasure of virtues which had come from heaven. Yet almost all those who saw or learned about the unusual and almost unheard of rigor of their life, instead of approaching them, hastened to avoid them in both spirit and body, nor did they cease from doubting in the ability of the monks to persevere. But the mercy of God, which inspired His own chosen ones to form this spiritual army did not cease to swell and to complete their ranks, to the profit of many, as the following will show.

XVII. *About the Death of the First Abbot and the Election of the Second and Their Institutes and Their Happiness*

The man of the Lord, Alberic, however, after he had practiced fruitfully regular discipline in the school of Christ for nine and a half years, went home to the Lord, full of glory in his faith and virtues, and therefore deservedly to be rewarded by God with eternal life. His successor was a certain brother by the name of Stephen, an Englishman by nationality, who had also come to that place with the others from Molesme, a lover of the Rule and of the place. During his time, the brethren and this abbot prohibited the duke of that land or any other lord from keeping his court at any time in that monastery as they used in times past to do on the occasion of great feasts. Furthermore, lest anything remain in the house of God—where it was their wish to serve God devoutly day and night—that savored of pride or superfluity or that would ever corrupt poverty, the safeguard of virtues, which they had chosen of their own free will, they resolved to keep no crosses of gold or silver but only painted wooden ones; no candelabra, but only one of iron; no thuribles, but only of copper and iron; no chasubles, but of fustian or linen, without a pallium of gold or silver; no albs or amices but of linen, similarly without a pallium of gold or silver. They gave up entirely the use of all pallia and copes as well as dalmatics and tunics. But they retained the use of chalices of silver or, where possible, of gold-plate, but not ones of pure gold; and the communion reed of silver or, where possible, of gold-plate; stoles as well as maniples of silk only, without gold and silver. Moreover they explicitly ordered that altar cloths be made of plain linen and without ornamentation and that the cruets be without gold and silver.

In those days the monastery increased in its possession of lands, vineyards, meadows and granges; but it did not decrease in religious fervor. Therefore in those days God visited that place and showed forth His deepest mercy to the brethren who implored Him, who cried out to Him, and who wept before Him, who day and night groaned long and deep, who drew near the brink of despair because they had almost no successors. For now the grace of God sent to that monastery so many literate and noble clerics and laymen who were as powerful as they were distinguished in the world that at one time thirty men eagerly entered the cell of novices, and by fighting bravely and strongly against their own vices and the temptation of evil spirits, they completed their course. Through the example of these men who were old and young, men of every age group in diverse parts of the world were encouraged, since they saw through these that what they had feared impossible in the observance of the Rule was, indeed, possible. They started to flock together there in order to place their proud necks under the sweet yoke of Christ, to love fervently the rigorous and burdensome precepts of the Rule, and they began to make that community wonderfully happy and strong.

XVIII. About the Abbeys

From that time forward they established abbeys in various dioceses, which under the Lord's rich and powerful blessing so prospered from day to day that within eight years among those who had gone forth from Cîteaux itself and those who in turn sprang forth from them, twelve new foundations were to be counted.

The Exordium of Cîteaux

The Exordium of Cîteaux is a short historical introduction to a synopsis of the Charter of Charity. It was composed probably a short time after the abbots in Chapter at Cîteaux in 1123 accepted the Charter.

I. Departure of the Cistercian Monks from Molesme

In the diocese of Langres there lay, as is well known, a monastery by the name of Molesme; it was of great renown and outstanding in religious fervor. Within a short time of its foundation God in his goodness enriched it with the gift of his graces, raised it to honor with the presence of distinguished men, and caused it to be as great in possessions as it was resplendent in virtues. But, because possessions and virtues are not usually steady companions, several members of that holy community, men truly wise and filled with higher aspirations, decided to pursue heavenly studies rather than to be entangled in earthly affairs. Accordingly, these lovers of virtue soon came to think about that poverty which is fruitful to man. They realized that, although life in that place was a godly and upright life, they observed the Rule, which they had vowed to keep, in a way short of their desire and intention. They spoke amongst themselves and asked one another how they were to fulfill the verse: "I will fulfill my vows to you, vows which I made with my own lips" [Ps. 63:13]. What more needs to be said? After common deliberation, together with the father of that monastery, Robert of blessed memory, twenty-one monks went out to try to carry out jointly what they had conceived with one spirit. Eventually, after many labors and extreme difficulties, which all who wish to devote their life to Christ must endure, they reached their goal. They came to Cîteaux, which was then a place of horror, a vast wilderness. Realizing that the asperity of the place accorded well with the strict design they had already conceived [in their minds], the soldiers of Christ found the place, almost as though divinely prepared, to be as alluring as their design had been dear.

II. Beginnings of the Monastery of Cîteaux

Thus in the year 1098 of the Incarnation of Our Lord, supported with the counsel and strengthened with the authority of the venerable Hugh, archbishop of the church of Lyons, and at the time legate of the Apostolic See, and of the God-fearing man, Walter, bishop of Chalon, and of Odo, the illustrious duke of Burgundy, these men began to transform the solitude they had found into an abbey; abbot Robert received the care of the monks and the shepherd's staff from the bishop of the diocese; and under him the others vowed stability in that place. But, after a short time it happened that the same abbot Robert was reclaimed by the monks of Molesme, and was returned to Molesme on the order of Pope Urban II and with the permission and consent of Walter, bishop of Chalon. He was replaced by Alberic, a religious and holy man. For the sake of peace this wise agreement was made between the monasteries and confirmed by the pope: henceforth neither of them would [permanently] accept the other's monk without a proper recommendation. Through the solicitude and industry of its new father and with God's generous assistance, the New Monastery thereafter advanced in holiness, excelled in fame, and witnessed the increase of its temporal goods. The man of God, Alberic, who successfully ran his race for nine years [Phil. 2:16], obtained the crown of eternity in the tenth year. He was succeeded by the lord Stephen, an Englishman by nationality, an ardent lover of and staunch champion of religious life, poverty, and regular discipline. In his days the words of Scripture came true: "The eyes of the Lord are upon the just and His ears hear their prayer" [Ps. 33:16]. The little flock voiced its one and only complaint: that it was small in number. As I said, the "poor of Christ" came to fear and to dread almost to the point of despair one thing alone: that they might not be able to leave behind heirs to their poverty. For their neighbors applauded their holy life but abhorred its austerity and thus kept from imitating the men whose fervor they approved. Yet God, who can easily make great things from small ones and many things from a few, beyond all expectation, so aroused the hearts of many to the imitation of these monks that in the cell where the novices are tested, thirty had come to live under the same discipline: clerics as well as laymen, even nobles and men of power in the eyes of the world. Upon this so sudden and happy heavenly visitation the barren one which had no offspring began, not without reason, to rejoice: "Once forsaken, she now came to have many sons" [Is. 54:1]. And God did not cease to multiply His people, and to increase their joy, so that within about twelve years the happy mother came to see twenty abbots, drawn from her own sons as well as from the sons of her sons, like olive branches around her table. Indeed she did not think it out of order to follow the example of the holy Father Benedict whose Rule she embraced. Hence, as soon as the new plantation began to produce offshoots, blessed Father Stephen in his watchful wisdom provided a document of admirable discretion; it served as a trimming knife which was to cut off the outgrowth of division which, if unchecked, could suffocate the fruit of mutual peace. Very appropriately, he wished the document to be called a Charter of Charity, for, clearly, its whole content so breathed love that almost nothing else is seen to be treated there than this: "Owe no man anything but to love one another [Rom. 13:8]. This charter, arranged by the same father and confirmed by the aforementioned twenty abbots, was also approved by apostolic authority.

The Charter of Charity

The original Charter of Charity (now called Carta caritatis prior) was probably drafted by Saint Stephen Harding for papal approval in 1119. The Charter went through a long evolution, without losing its original spirit, especially in the years just prior to 1165 when the text we offer here (called Carta caritatis posterior) was final-ized. This is the text which guided the Cistercians through the cen-turies.

Before the Cistercian abbeys began to flourish, the lord abbot Stephen and his brethren, seeking to avoid any scandal between a bishop and the monks, ordained that no abbey should be founded in the diocese of any bishop before he approved and confirmed the decree enacted between the abbey of Cîteaux and its filiations. Anxi-ous to avert a future wreck of their mutual concord, in this decree the aforementioned brethren made clear, ordained and recorded for their successors by what bond, in what way, and, most importantly, by what charity their monks, scattered in body throughout abbeys in diverse parts of the world, should be indissolubly joined together in spirit. They also decided that this decree should be called a Char-ter of Charity, for its statutes, spurning the burden of heavy exac-tion, related only to charity and the welfare of souls in things human and divine.

1. Since we realize that we are servants, albeit unprofitable ones, of the one true King, our Lord and Master, we impose no exaction of temporal possessions or earthly goods on our fellow-abbots and fellow-monks and brothers whom, in diverse regions, the goodness of God has placed under the discipline of the Rule, to be cared for by us the least among men. For, wishing to be of service to them

and to all the children of Holy Church, we make no provision that would burden them, that would diminish their temporal goods, lest while seeking to enrich ourselves from their poverty we ourselves should fail to avoid the evil of avarice which, according to the Apostle, is the service of idols.

2. We do wish, however, to retain the care of their souls for the sake of charity so that if they should ever attempt, even if but in a small measure, to stray from their sacred resolve and the observance of the holy Rule—which may God avert—through our solicitude they may be able to return to the right path of life.

3. Now, therefore, we will and command them to observe the Rule of blessed Benedict in every particular just as it is observed in New Monastery; not to introduce any other interpretation into the text of the Holy Rule; but to understand it and to keep it just as our ancestors, our holy fathers, namely the monks of New Monastery, understood it and kept it, and as we, ourselves, understand it and keep it today. And because we receive all monks coming from other monasteries into ours, and they in like manner receive ours, it seems proper to us and it is, furthermore, our will that all our monasteries have usages in chanting and all the books necessary for day and night offices and the celebration of Masses similar to the usages and books in use at New Monastery; that there may be no discord in our daily actions, but that we may all live together in the bond of charity under one rule and in the practice of the same usages.

4. No monastery or person of our Order shall undertake to request a privilege contrary to the common regulations of the Order from anyone or, if already obtained, retain it under any pretext.

5. Whenever the Abbot of New Monastery comes to visit any one of these monasteries, in order to acknowledge that the abbey of New Monastery is the mother of his abbey, the local abbot shall yield his place to the visitor, everywhere in the monastery, and the visiting abbot shall hold the place of the local abbot as long as he stays there, with one exception: he shall not eat in the guest-house but in the refectory, for the sake of preserving monastic discipline, unless the local abbot is absent. All other visiting abbots of our Order shall do likewise. But, if several abbots come and the local abbot is absent, the senior of them shall eat in the guest-house. Another exception is this: the local abbot will bless his own novices after the regular period of probation, even if a senior abbot is present.

6. The abbot of New Monastery shall also take care not to presume to treat nor to ordain anything about the affairs of the monastery he is visiting, against the wishes of the abbot and the brethren. If, however, he finds that the precepts of the Rule or of our Order are violated in that place, he shall charitably strive to correct the brethren with the advice of the local abbot. If, however, the local abbot is not present, the visitor shall nevertheless correct what he finds amiss.

7. Once a year the abbot of the mother-house shall visit all the monasteries that he himself has founded, either in person or through one of his co-abbots. And if he visits the brethren more often, then let them rejoice the more.

8. The four proto-abbots—the abbots of La Ferté, Pontigny, Clairvaux and Morimond—shall jointly visit the monastery of Cîteaux, unless one of them is prevented by grave illness, on a day appointed by them, other than when they are attending the yearly chapter.

9. If any abbot of our Order comes to New Monastery due reverence shall be shown to him. If the abbot [of New Monastery] is absent, the visitor shall occupy his stall; he shall receive guests; he shall eat with them in the guest-house. But if the abbot [of New Monastery] is present, the visitor shall do none of these things; rather he shall eat in the refectory. The local prior shall manage the affairs of the monastery.

10. Between abbeys not bound by filiation this will be the law: Every abbot shall yield his place everywhere in his own monastery to a visiting fellow-abbot so that Scripture may be fulfilled: "They give one another precedence with honor" [Rom. 12:10]. If two or more abbots arrive, the senior of the guests will occupy the first place. All shall eat in the refectory, except the local abbot, just as we have said above. Wherever else they meet, seniority will be according to the antiquity of their abbeys, so that the abbot of the older house will occupy the first place. As soon as they take their seats, they shall bow to each other.

11. If by the grace of God any of our houses shall so increase that it is able to found another monastery, they too shall observe among themselves the agreement which we observe with our brethren, except that they shall not hold general chapters among themselves.

12. Instead, all abbots of our Order will, putting aside all excuses, meet annually in general chapter, except those who are prevented by bodily infirmity; these will depute a suitable representative through whom the reason for staying away may be reported to the chapter. Excepted also are those who live in distant regions; they shall come at intervals to be decided for them in the chapter. But if any abbot presumes to stay away from the general chapter for any other reason whatsoever, he shall ask pardon in the chapter of the following year and he shall not leave without a severe punishment.

13. In the chapter, the abbots shall discuss matters pertaining to the salvation of their souls, and ordain what is to be corrected or added in the observance of the holy Rule and the regulations of the Order. They shall also strengthen one another in the bond of peace and charity.

14. If any abbot is found to be less than zealous about the Rule, or too involved in secular affairs, or faulty in any matter, he shall be charitably accused at the chapter; upon his accusation, he shall ask pardon and do the penance imposed on him for his fault. Only abbots shall make such an accusation.

15. If, perchance, a controversy arises among any of the abbots, or so grievous a fault is charged against any one of them that he would deserve suspension or even deposition, whatever is decreed by the chapter in this matter shall be observed without hesitation.

16. If, however, a case turns into discord because of a difference of views, then the decision of the abbot of Cîteaux and of those who appear to be of wiser counsel and more suitable character shall be observed inviolably, subject to this observation: that no one of those abbots who is involved specifically in the case ought to participate in the determination of the case.

17. If any monastery incurs unbearable poverty, the abbot of that monastery shall strive to reveal this plight to the entire chapter. Then, inflamed by the fire of charity, the assembled abbots shall take quick steps to relieve the poverty of that monastery according to their ability, from the goods which God has given them.

18. If any monastery of our Order is without its own abbot, the Father-Abbot of that house shall assume its administration until a new abbot is elected. When a date of election has been fixed, the abbots whom that house has sent forth—if there are any—shall be

summoned, and, according to the counsel and will of the Father-Abbot, the abbots and the monks of that house shall elect an abbot.

19. Whenever Cîteaux is without her own abbot, because she is the mother of all our monasteries, the four proto-abbots—the abbots of La Ferté, Pontigny, Clairvaux and Morimond—shall make the necessary provisions. They shall be in charge of that house until an abbot has been duly elected and confirmed.

20. At least fifteen days before a date has been appointed and announced for the election of an abbot of Cîteaux, there shall be summoned those abbots whose houses sprang from Cîteaux and other abbots whom the aforesaid abbots and brethren of Cîteaux know to be of suitable character. Then, assembled in the name of the Lord, the abbots and monks of Cîteaux shall elect an abbot.

21. Also, any mother-abbey shall be allowed freely to receive an abbot not only from the monks of her daughter-monasteries, but from the abbots if it should be necessary.

22. But none of our monasteries shall elect a person of another order as its abbot, just as none of our monasteries is permitted to give an abbot to other monasteries which are not of our Order.

23. If an abbot, because of his inefficiency or timidity, asks his Father-Abbot, from whose house his own has gone forth, to be released from the burden of his abbacy, the Father-Abbot shall be careful not to consent easily and without a well-founded and compelling reason. But even if the reason is sufficiently great, the Father-Abbot shall not do anything in the matter of his own, but after having summoned other abbots of our Order he shall undertake with their counsel whatever they together judge ought to be done.

24. But if it becomes public knowledge that any abbot despises the holy Rule or sins against our Order, or acquiesces in the faults of the brethren entrusted to his care, the abbot of the mother-house shall, either in person or through the prior of his own monastery or in any other more suitable way, admonish him up to four times to correct his ways. But if he neither will be corrected in this way nor resign voluntarily, an assembly of a number of other abbots of our congregation shall remove the transgressor of the holy Rule from his office. Then, according to the counsel and the will of the abbot of the mother-abbey, a new abbot who is worthy shall be elected by the monks of that house and the abbots of its filiation, if there are any, in the manner described above.

25. If, however—which may God forbid—a deposed abbot or his monks choose to be contumacious and rebellious and altogether refuse to accept the sentence [of deposition], they shall be placed under excommunication by the abbot of the mother-house and his co-abbots; and from that time forward they shall be restrained to the extent that he is able and that he sees fit.

26. But if afterwards anyone of those evildoers, having returned to his senses, should wish to call his dead soul back to life and to return to his mother-abbey, he shall be received as a repentant son.

27. Except for this reason—and every effort must be made that this not come about—no abbot shall retain the monk of another abbot without the latter's consent; nor shall an abbot send his own monks to live in the house of another abbot without the latter's consent.

28. Similarly as well—and may this never happen—if, perchance the abbots of our Order learn that Cîteaux, our mother, has grown tepid in her holy endeavor and strayed from the observance of the Rule and of our Order, the four proto-abbots—those of La Ferté, Pontigny, Clairvaux and Morimond—shall admonish the abbot of that place in the name of the other abbots, up to four times, to mend his ways and to take care to correct the conduct of his charges. In addition they shall zealously implement the other measures prescribed for abbots who prove themselves incorrigible, with this exception: If the abbot of Cîteaux refuses to resign voluntarily, they can neither depose him nor excommunicate him until they depose the unprofitable man from his office in the general chapter or, if in their judgment things cannot wait that long, in another assembly comprising the abbots of Cîteaux's filiation and certain other abbots who had been summoned. Then both the abbots and the monks of Cîteaux shall strive to elect a suitable abbot.

29. But if that abbot and the monks of Cîteaux in their pride choose to resist, the abbots shall not fear to strike them with the sword of excommunication.

30. But if afterwards any of these prevaricators, regaining his senses and anxious to save his soul, should seek refuge in any of these four houses—La Ferté, Pontigny, Clairvaux and Morimond—he shall be received in satisfaction of the Rule as a member and fellow-heir of the house, until he is restored to his own monastery upon its reconciliation, as justice demands. During this period, however, the yearly chapter of abbots will not be held at Cîteaux, but wherever the four proto-abbots shall determine.

The Epistle of Thurstan of York

The Letter of Thurstan, Archbishop of York, to William of Corbeil, the Archbishop of Canterbury and Legate of the Apostolic See, gives a very colorful and sometimes amusing account of the events which set the stage for the founding of Fountains Abbey. The Letter was written in the last months of 1132. No less a person than Bernard of Clairvaux proclaims the merits of the author, Archbishop Thurstan:

> The splendor of your work and your reputation among men have combined greatly, as I know, to your credit. Your deeds prove that yours is no undeserved or empty reputation, for facts themselves bear out what hitherto has everywhere been reported of you . . . I admire you. . . .

Thurston not only had a great understanding and appreciation of monastic life, as is seen in this letter, but also a personal desire to embrace it, as is evident from another letter addressed to him by St. Bernard. Thurstan's Letter is brought forward as a witness to the fact that the Cistercian Fathers sought to live the evangelical life according to the monastic tradition expressed in the Rule of St. Benedict.

Thurstan repeatedly and explicitly states that this was the intent of the Founders of Fountains Abbey:

> . . . men who were determined to correct their way of life according to the Rule of St. Benedict, or rather, according to the truth of the Gospel.(3)
>
> These brethren with many tears sought nothing but . . . that they might not be impeded from living in evangelical peace and observing the Rule of the Blessed Father Benedict.(4)

All of them are seeking full observance of the Rule and of their profession and likewise of the Gospel.(19)

. . . these men who wish truly to obey the Gospel of Christ and the Rule of St. Benedict . . .(20)

The Epistle of Thurstan, Archbishop of York

To William his most revered Lord in Christ's love, by the grace of God Archbishop of Canterbury and Legate of the Apostolic See, Thurstan, by the same grace, Archbishop of York, expresses the earnest desire that his Lord might grow in Christ and never fall away.

1. It is the highest honor of an ecclesiastical dignitary to give the best counsel to the finest sons of the Church when they are in most difficult situations. Wherefore, my venerable Lord and esteemed Father, we have decided to bring to the attention of your Paternity an unusual thing which has happened recently among us here at York.

2. Indeed, it is well known and certain to many men how great in the eyes of all is the goodness and virtuous renown of the outstanding Monastery of St. Mary's of York. Because it is without doubt true that when riches increase, virtue begins to wane and be less constant, some of the brethren of this monastery for the past half-year, moved by divine inspiration I believe, have begun to be very concerned about the manner and condition of their way of life. The gnawing of their consciences, as they have testified, has caused them much distress. For they fear that they would be wholly failing if they did not live out in a holy way their awesome vows. Whence, these brethren of York were struck with a very terrible fear in that they seemed to carry out their profession in nothing, or, at least, in very few things. They feared, indeed, lest they were running or had run, if indeed not to damnation itself, at least in vain because of the guilt that lay upon them for such great infidelity to their vows. They believed it to be a crime, or rather insanity, to bear the yoke of the Rule of St. Benedict not unto salvation but unto condemnation.

3. Therefore, disturbed by these things, these brethren undertook to make known the concern that was burning in their hearts to their Prior, Richard, revealing their fear concerning their transgressions. They sought his help to correct the situation; and lest he fear to be of help out of considerations of prosperity or adversity, they ad-

jured him by the Spirit of God and the Name of Christ. He was alarmed at the novelty of the thing they offered. But although among his own his position was the best, once he heard the quiet call to a better life, he pondered seriously upon the doubtful promise of his transitory good fortune. For a short time he took counsel within himself, considering the alternatives, and then he made his decision. He promised not only to help, but, indeed, to ally himself with their desires. What then? Within a short time the number increased to fully thirteen who were determined to correct their way of life according to the Rule of St. Benedict, or rather, according to the truth of the Gospel.

4. Therefore, on the Vigil of the holy Apostles Peter and Paul, our beloved brother, Prior Richard, on whom almost the whole care of the monastery rested, taking with him his Subprior, Gervaise, who was well known among his brethren for his religious spirit, went to their Lord Abbot and frankly made known to him the whole matter as it had developed. The Lord Abbot, a man who, in his own way and according to his own lights, is decent and good, but, however, overly simple and unschooled, was terrified by the miracle of this new spirit. He denied that he could change in his monastery the ancient rites and the usual practices which generally obtained throughout the whole world. But the Prior, as a man well read, responded: "Father, we do not seek to introduce anything crude or new. We must undertake with all our strength to observe by God's grace the true and age-old service of our blessed Father Benedict, or rather, the more ancient Gospel of Christ, which precedes all vows and rules. We do not seek to detract in any way from the rest of the monks. We are not envious of their practices. We know that in every place one Lord is served. We fight under one King. Both in the public square and in the cloister the same grace of God prevails and wins out. For Job is stronger on his dungheap than Adam in Paradise. Whatever the blessed Benedict established, the whole of it was designed by the Providence of the Holy Spirit, so that nothing more useful, more holy, or happy can be conceived. As he knew and taught that idleness was the enemy of the soul, he arranged that certain times should be given to reading and to fervent prayer and that certain times be given to labor and to work, in such wise that at one time the soul would be fruitfully employed, at another, the body, and thus both would be saved from weariness. And, moreover, he added this, 'Coarse jests and idle words or words that move to laughter,

these we exclude forever from every part of the cloister. For such speech we do not permit the disciple to open his mouth.' And in another place he says: 'At all times a monk should be zealous for silence, but especially during the night hours.' How diligently this decree has been observed is not unknown to anyone who knows our practices. For while some are going to church after collation, others step aside to jest and to exchange useless and garrulous talk, as if the evil of the day were not sufficient, unless there were added to it that of the night.''

5. He added many things, moreover, concerning the delicate food, the sweet and expensive variety of drinks, the expensive quality of the clothes. "This was not the taste of our blessed Father Benedict; it was not what he taught. He did not attend to the color of the clothes but to the needed warmth. He did not look after the tastiness of the vegetables. Rather, necessity was hardly satisfied by frugality. St. Benedict acknowledges as his own only those who live in the monastery under a rule and an abbot. So, venerable Father, if you will allow, we will hasten back to the purity of the Gospel, to evangelical perfection and peace. For we see that nothing or very little shines forth in our conduct and in our actions which was taught by Christ. We are filled with concupiscence, we are angry, we quarrel, we steal from others, we go to court to get our goods back, we defend ourselves with fraud and lies, we follow the ways of the flesh and its desires, we live for ourselves, we please ourselves, we fear being overcome, we glory in overcoming others, we oppress others and seek to avoid being oppressed, we envy others and we glory in our own perfections, we take our pleasure, grow fat on the sweat of others, and the whole world does not suffice for our wickedness. It seems as if the Gospel had perished and become impossible for us.

6. "We think of the monks of Savigny and Clairvaux who recently came to us. The Gospel so clearly shone out in them that it must be said it would be more useful to imitate them than to recite it. When, indeed, their holy life is seen, it is as if the Gospel were being relived in them. They alone do not seek their own. They alone possess nothing by which they would seek to prefer themselves to their brethren. They alone do not seek the harm of their neighbors. They are content to cultivate a little land and to use some cattle. And these things, indeed, they do not desire to have except insofar as God wills it. Because when God wills to take them away from them they do

not seek to keep them. For them, if I be not mistaken, it is fitting to say: 'The world is crucified to us and we to the world.' For them it is fitting to say: 'Forgive us our trespasses as we forgive those who trespass against us,' because they have no trespasser from whom they wish to demand anything. Happy, indeed, are men such as these whose clothing, food, and whole way of life savor of the Gospel. Their portion is God alone. They know, insofar as it is humanly possible, how to be filled with the love of God and neighbor. Adhering to God alone, they so fully leave behind all temporal things except for a poor contemptible habit, they desire nothing over which a neighbor could become angry."

7. "Therefore, Father, never let it seem to be impossible to hold fast to the Rule of St. Benedict, as long as God gives us such examples as these who go before us in the way of holiness and virtue so that we may follow them. If, indeed, because of the nearness and the noisiness of the people we are not able wholly to follow them, let us at least advert to our way of life and profession according to our Rule, and moreover, to the fact that we are not monks but rather dead men."

8. In this manner, the Lord Prior, Richard, spoke with their Lord Abbot, Geoffrey, concerning the reformation of their monastery. The Lord Abbot did not receive these words with joy because it is difficult to change long standing practices.

9. Nevertheless, confessing himself to be unlearned and less perspicacious, he asked if he might be more fully informed in writing as to how such things could be accomplished in his monastery. Prior Richard willingly accepted this and was not slow in fulfilling it. He wrote that they ought to conform to what the Rule permitted in speech, clothes, and food. He so carefully explained the arrangement and order of the monastery that it seemed as if the Rule could be observed in the city hardly less perfectly than in a desert. Knowing secular affairs well, he arranged their temporalities with such fidelity that he in no way departed from evangelical justice. Everything concerning the incomes from churches and tithes, in regard to the investment of which monks are usually held to be more reprehensible, was to be undertaken and done with the legitimate and canonical advice of the bishops, and they were to be used only for the poor, the pilgrims, and for guests. He decreed that the monks were to live by agriculture and the rearing of cattle.

10. When the rumor of all these things began to reach the others, the anger of the rest of the community burst forth in a jealous rage. They thought that this man and his companions should be sent into exile or thrown into prison.

11. After meeting with them many times in different places for friendly talks, the Lord Abbot saw that only with difficulty could he change what his predecessors seemed to have upheld. Nevertheless, wishing in this matter to use good counsel, he put off a full reply until after the Nativity of the Blessed Virgin Mary. Meanwhile, some of the brethren, vainly fearing that they were to be constricted by more than the regular discipline, began, out of envy toward the Prior and the others, to plot like the Pharisees. If the benignity of some had not brought about a delay, immediate persecution would have burst out.

12. At the same time the rumor of the internal strife spread among the people outside. We heard this talk among the people, but the truth of the matter remained hidden. Then Prior Richard, bringing with him the Subprior and the Secretary of the monastery, came to make the truth of the situation known to us. They sought the clemency of St. Peter and of ourselves in order that they might begin without delay to undertake to observe what they had vowed. They said their need was pressing, especially because the brethren had so conspired that if any one of them said anything about his profession he would be excommunicated. Some of the companions of the Prior, shaken by fear or self-love or vanity, so turned back because they could not otherwise find peace, that they confessed it as a fault that they had said anything about observing their profession.

13. Therefore, I, Thurstan, by the grace of God, Archbishop of York, heard these servants of Christ who, according to the command of St. Benedict, wished to prefer nothing to the love of Christ. I feared to offend in them Christ's grace if I did not receive their just petition with pastoral concern. It pertains to the primary responsibilities of a bishop to provide for monks a sacred peace and to comfort the oppressed in their need. Therefore, taking the advice of holy men, I convoked the Lord Abbot Geoffrey and the Prior Richard with his Subprior to a suitable place in order that with some other holy men I might peacefully receive the petition of the brethren and the reply of the Abbot.

14. These brothers, with many tears, sought nothing but what they had previously asked, namely, that they might follow the poor Christ

in voluntary poverty, that they might carry the Cross of Christ in their own bodies, that they might not be impeded from living in evangelical peace and observing the Rule of the blessed Father Benedict. To do this, they earnestly sought the permission and the paternal help of their Lord Abbot. And, indeed, the Lord Abbot with tears confessed that their undertaking was something very much needed and he promised that he would not stand in the way of their desire, which was holy, but without the consent of his chapter he dared not promise anything in regard to the assistance they sought.

15. And so the Lord Abbot returned to the monastery with his monks. In the meantime there was peace and a day was established on which I would come to their chapter and, with some religious who would come with me, would treat with the Abbot on this matter. Meanwhile, the rest of the brethren displayed their envy with increasing cruelty as these men sought more manifestly to carry out their desire. They called in some men from the Great Abbey and some monks of Cluny who were dwelling in the neighborhood. And in their presence and with their approval they deprived these monks, as men who had profaned and deserted the common order, of every dignity and responsibility in the monastery, for, after the Abbot, the greatest responsibility in the monastery had been in their hands. All of this happened in the interim.

16. On the established day, early in the morning, I prepared to come to the chapter of the monks. I had almost arrived at the very door—with me there were a number of wise and religious men: Hugh, the Deacon; William, the Prior of the Clerks Regular of Cisbarne; William, the Treasurer; Hugh, the Archdeacon; Serlo, the Canon; Alfred, my Chaplain and Canon; and Robert, the Chaplain of the Hospital. We had left our horses outside the inner gate with a few men.

17. Then, as I have said, as we were about to enter the door of the chapter, the Lord Abbot met us at the door with his monks, who fairly filled the chapter room. He forbade me to enter unless some of the clerics who were with me were sent away. I was scarcely able to reply that I ought not to enter upon such an affair without my clerics who were good and wise men and their friends, when, behold, the whole chapter resounded with shouting and terrible cries. It seemed that I was faced with the seditious outburst of drunken and debauched men rather than with the humility of monks, of which nothing was there. Many rose up, and swinging their arms as if they

would charge to the attack, cried that they would leave if I entered. I said: "God is my witness, that I came as a Father, with no thought of inflicting harm on you, desiring only that there be peace and Christian fraternity among you. Now, in truth, because you have sought to take away from me what pertains to the episcopal authority and office, I, in like manner, take from you what you need. I place your church under interdict." Then one of them, Simon by name, said: "We would prefer to have our church a hundred years under interdict." To this all assented and cried in upraised voices: "Seize them!" Seizing the Prior and his companions, they began to pull them away, wishing, as they had decided among themselves, either to throw them into prison or to send them into exile. The latter, indeed, having no other hope of escaping their hands, clung to me, looking for the peace of Peter and our peace. So we ran to the church, and they, all the way, screamed and cried: "Seize the rebels! Apprehend the traitors!" Thus we escaped into the church. The Abbot and the rest of his monks returned to their chapter.

18. While this was going on, the men of the Abbey stood around the closed doors and the entrance gates as if lying in ambush. We (as I must truly confess), fearing an attack from the monks, took care to bar, from within, the door of the church which opened on the cloister. Meanwhile, the news spread abroad and people gathered, but no untoward thing was said or done by them.

19. Since, therefore, nothing could be done to establish concord among the monks, we returned home, taking with us the group: twelve priests and a subdeacon. Several of them are learned men. All are seeking full observance of the Rule and their profession and likewise of the Gospel. And so they dwelt as guests in the house of St. Peter, our residence. They are in no wise deterred from their proposal by the violence they have suffered. However, the brethren of the abbey, on their part, carry on without restraint, and the Abbot—I know not for what reason—has gone off on a journey.

20. Wherefore, we beseech your paternity, in Christ, to defend with your authority the interests of these monks who desire to change to a stricter and more austere life. If, in fact, their Abbot comes to you, guide him back to peace with your God-given authority and wisdom, and warn him not to impede the holy resolution of his sons. If he has already come and gone, we ask that through the present messenger you send letters to him, exhorting him not to stand perti-

naciously against these men, who wish truly to obey the Gospel of Christ and the Rule of St. Benedict, but rather to give them his assistance and the opportunity to do as they desire. The Abbot and his monks ought at least in this to imitate the Egyptians and the Babylonians, who allowed the Israelites to go in quest of the Land of Promise. Indeed, when Jacob secretly fled from Laban's domination, Laban, after a cruel persecution, let him return to his fatherland. In truth, they are not to be thought deserters but prudent men who wish to leave a place where there is greater liberty to sin, desiring one where they can live more safely in communion with God. Indeed, Christ himself threatens them! Did he not rebuke the Pharisees in that they themselves did not enter, and would not permit others to enter? It is indeed known to all that the Rule of St. Benedict commonly, and it might be said almost everywhere in the world, has lost its proper place and observance in almost everything. Really, no one can be sufficiently amazed that some dare to promise before God and his saints with such solemnity that which they will daily neglect, or, if I might speak more truly, will be compelled not to observe. What the prophet says fits them perfectly: "This people honors me with their lips, but their heart is far from me." And, as the Apostle says: "They confess with their voice to know God but in their deeds they deny him."

21. Perhaps it is true that many act in this way. Frequency makes for audacity. Truly, I must say in sorrow, it is deceived, it is wholly deceived, this audacity of the monks, because a multitude of sins does not grant impunity to the sinners. Wherefore, those who wish to observe the Rule of their profession are not to be impeded but to be protected. They are not to be reprehended when, for this reason, they hasten to change their place, for God is not chosen for the sake of a place. The place is chosen for the sake of God. St. Benedict clearly testifies that in every place it is the same Lord God who is served, the same King for whom the battle is fought. In the Conferences of the Fathers, the hermit Joseph said very clearly that that man was more faithful to his profession who went where he could more fully live out the precepts of the Lord of faith. And, indeed, "He who helps us in our needs and in our tribulations helps us to seek a holy situation." If I be not mistaken, they should be considered Pharisees and heretics who do not fear nor permit others to fear what Truth himself has said: "Unless your justice exceeds

that of the Scribes and the Pharisees, you will not enter the kingdom of heaven.'' For, if an angel from heaven preaches other than that which must be preached, let him be anathema. And he preaches a Gospel other than Christ's Gospel who tries to impede men who seek angelic peace and the observance of the Rule of their profession. Whoever he be, he must be totally refuted, as Truth himself says: "If your right eye scandalize you, tear it out and cast if from you." Nothing in the body causes more pain when it is wounded, or is more carefully taken care of, than the eye. Nevertheless, when it becomes an impediment, it must be spiritually torn out. For this is the prudence of the serpent, to free the head—that is, the mind— from all folly that can wound the soul.

22. Because of the scandal of the weak, who have less ability to discern the truth, we ask Your Holiness and all who wish to hear this petition of ours, to endeavor, insofar as it is possible, to restore peace between the Abbot of York and these brothers. We ought to recall what happened in the affair of the Molesme monks, which is quite similar. The Cistercians went forth to establish and found a most perfect way of life which has set the whole Church at wonder. The Lord Hugh, of venerable memory, the Archbishop of Lyons, with true Christian piety praised the extraordinary purity of their life. They faithfully undertook a renewal of the Holy Rule and a total living of it. And then, when complaints of the jealous came to the knowledge of the Apostolic See, Pope Urban II issued a decree to the effect that as long as the Abbot returned to his duties as Abbot in his former monastery, none of the others who wished to persevere in a full living of the Rule should suffer any impediment or molestation. Indeed, it is clearer than light that in their wonderful way of life the truth of the whole Gospel shines forth.

23. We have been very long, and perhaps tiresome, in this letter. But, although it will not please them, it seemed that the situation of the monks remaining at St. Mary's should be clearly set forth, lest only the opinion of these jealous men be known, which should not be the case.

24. May Your Holiness prosper in Christ.

Declaration of the General Chapter of 1969 on the Cistercian Life

We Cistercian monks feel a deep desire to interpret for our own times the traditions which our Fathers have handed down to us. Yet we must admit that we are faced with a variety of different trends in our Order which reflect its present situation. We may feel at times that certain of these trends could well obstruct the renewal and healthy evolution of the Order.

And yet, when these difficulties came to light at the opening of this Chapter for renewal, we all felt a profound sense of communion in the lived experience of our common spiritual values. We are convinced that the work of this Chapter will become constructive to the degree that we foster this communion and the mutual confidence which it inspires.

We shall do this by recognizing all that really unites us in the Holy Spirit rather than by trying to impose unity through a legislation that would determine observances down to the last detail. Individual communities can, in fact, look after such details according to local needs and in conformity with the directives of the General Chapter—so long as our wholly contemplative orientation is maintained. We are convinced that the best laws are those which follow and interpret life and it is in the concrete experience of our Cistercian vocation that we would first of all recognize this life.

Our wish is to clarify the content of this experience which we all share and by so doing to further as best we can the values which inspire it. That is why we feel moved to make the following declaration on our own particular way of life:

> Following the first Fathers of our Order, we find in the Holy Rule of St. Benedict the practical interpretation of the Gospel for us.

A sense of the Divine Transcendence and of the Lordship of Christ not only pervades the whole of this Rule but also permeates our life, totally orientated towards an experience of the Living God. God calls and we respond by truly seeking him as we follow Christ in humility and obedience. With hearts cleansed by the Word of God, by vigils, by fasting and by an unceasing conversion of life, we aim to become ever more disposed to receive from the Holy Spirit the gift of pure and continual prayer.

This search for God is the soul of our monastic day, a day composed of the *Opus Dei, lectio divina* and manual work. Our Cistercian life is basically simple and austere. It is truly poor and penitential "in the joy of the Holy Spirit." Through the warmth of their welcome and hospitality our communities share the fruit of their contemplation and work with others.

We carry out this search for God under a Rule and an abbot in a community of love where all are responsible. It is through stability that we commit ourselves to this community. It lives in an atmosphere of silence and separation from the world which fosters and expresses its openness to God in contemplation—treasuring, as Mary did, all these things and pondering them in her heart.

The Church has entrusted a mission to us which we wish to fulfill by the response of our whole life: "to give clear witness to the heavenly home for which every man longs and to keep alive in the heart of the human family the desire for this home . . . as we bear witness to the majesty and love of God and to the brotherhood of all men in Christ." (See *Gaudium et Spes,* no. 38; *Ad Gentes,* no. 40; Letter of Pope Paul VI to the Abbot General of the Order of Cîteaux, December 8, 1968).

Unity and Pluralism
A Statute of the General Chapter
of 1969

This present General Chapter is convinced that "the unity which is based on charity and which has been the strength and beauty of the Cistercian Order ever since its origins" (Letter of Paul VI to the Abbot General), will best be served today by a deep sense of communion in the lived experience of our common spiritual values. That is why the present Chapter, in its Declaration on the Cistercian Life, has already insisted on the contemplative orientation and fundamental observances of our Order.

In the present statute those observances which demand special attention in our times are presented in a more concrete fashion. Thus the fundamental values of our life are guaranteed without imposing a detailed uniformity where in fact a legitimate diversity should exist. Conditions are laid down so that each community, in union with the other monasteries of the Order and following these guidelines, may deepen its own living experience of the Cistercian life.

Guidelines

1. Faithful to the thought of their Founders, Cistercian monks live under a Rule and an abbot. They live, united in the love of Christ, in a community which is stable and effectively separated from the world.

2. The abbot, as spiritual father of his community, should try to discover the will of God. One important way of doing this is

by listening to his brethren in the spirit of Chapter Three of the Rule.

3. In our daily horarium we keep the balance between the *Opus Dei, lectio divina* and manual work as required by the Rule of St. Benedict.

4. The hour of rising is to be regulated so that vigils, which follows it, should keep its traditional character of nocturnal prayer—as we watch for the coming of the Lord.

5. The monk, who is tending to a life of continual prayer, needs a fixed amount of prayer each day. The abbot will see to this for the community as a whole or for each individual in particular.

6. This search for a life of prayer should be lived in an atmosphere of recollection and silence for which all are responsible. In particular, the great silence at night and the silence in the regular places will be maintained.

7. Separation from the world demands that journeys out of the monastery should be infrequent and only for serious reasons. The use of radio and television will be exceptional. Discretion is needed in the use of other media of communication.

8. Our monasteries should practice generous hospitality, but this should not be allowed to interfere with the contemplative nature of our way of life.

9. Our diet should be simple and frugal. The monastic practice of fasting and abstinence should be retained.

10. The habit is to be retained as the distinctive sign of the Order. Its use can differ from house to house.

11. The life of the community, as of each monk, should be marked by simplicity and poverty. Fraternal correction in the spirit of the Gospel is a help in this direction.

Constitutions and Statutes
of
The Cistercian Order
of the Strict Observance

approved by the General Chapter of 1987,
approved by the Holy See, June 3, 1990.

Part One: The Cistercian Patrimony

Cst 1. The Cistercian Tradition

1. The Cistercian Order of the Strict Observance has its origin in that monastic tradition of evangelical life which found expression in the *Rule for Monasteries* of Saint Benedict of Nursia. This Rule set forth a body of doctrine and practice which was gradually accepted throughout Latin monasticism, and which provides the foundation for the pursuit of our monastic ideal.

2. Saint Robert of Molesme, Saint Alberic and Saint Stephen Harding gave this tradition a more specific form when, in 1098, they established the New Monastery of Cîteaux, the Mother of us all, and founded the Cistercian Order. Around the year 1125 Saint Stephen also established the nuns' monastery of Tart as a true daughter house of Cîteaux, entrusted to the pastoral care of its abbot. The *Exordium Parvum* and the *Charter of Charity* are expressions of this vocation and mission which the founders received from God, and which the Church has authenticated both in their times and today. Under the influence of Saint Bernard of Clairvaux and others, the ideal of the

reform was propagated, so that monasteries of monks and nuns following the Cistercian way of life spread even beyond the boundaries of Western Europe. During this founding period the lay brothers and sisters became a feature of the Order. Through the lives and labors of innumerable brothers and sisters a substantial spiritual heritage was engendered which found expression in writing and in music, in architecture and in the arts, as well as in the skillful administration of their lands.

3. Monks and nuns of the Cistercian Order of the Strict Observance acknowledge their indebtedness to the movement which is called the Strict Observance, which strongly defended certain aspects of the Cistercian patrimony in difficult times, and made it possible for these values to be handed on to succeeding generations, largely through the work of Abbot de Rancé and the initiative of Dom Augustine de Lestranges. In 1892, three Congregations which traced their origins to La Valsainte united to form a single, autonomous Order, which they called the Order of Reformed Cistercians of Our Lady of La Trappe, and which now bears the name of the Cistercian Order of the Strict Observance.

4. The desire for an authentic monastic life, which is evident at so many points throughout this long history, continues to animate the monks and nuns of the Order in their vigorous efforts to renew their life. In obedience to the mandate of the Second Vatican Council they labor to arrive at a deeper understanding of their origins and, at the same time, to grow in docility to God's action in the present. The General Chapter of 1969, in its *Declaration on Cistercian Life* and its *Statute on Unity and Pluralism*, reaffirmed the Order's commitment to the Rule of Saint Benedict as a practical interpretation of the Gospel and gave guidelines for its faithful observance in the changed conditions of the world. In these documents the General Chapter distinguished between the orientation and fundamental observances of the Rule, which constitute the Cistercian way of life, and those details which can be modified according to local circumstances.

5. This collection of constitutions and statutes is the fruit of the experience of those years of renewal. It is very much to be hoped that they will be an effective instrument by the help of which the Order will be able to perfect itself in the spirit of the Second Vatican Council

and show itself ever more proficient in carrying out its particular role in the Church and in the world.

Cst 2. *The Nature and Purpose of the Order*

The monks and nuns of the Cistercian Order of the Strict Observance dedicate themselves entirely to God, giving themselves to him alone in a life which is monastic and contemplative, as this is defined in these Constitutions.

Cst 3. *The Spirit of the Order*

1. The Cistercian way of life is cenobitic. Cistercian monks seek God and follow Christ under a rule and an abbot, and form a stable community as a school of brotherly love. One in heart and mind, the brothers have all things in common. By bearing one another's burdens they fulfill the law of Christ, and sharing in his suffering they hope to find entry into the kingdom of heaven.

2. The monastery is a school of the Lord's service, where Christ is formed in the hearts of the brothers through the liturgy, the teaching of the abbot and the fraternal way of life. Through God's word, the monks are trained in a discipline of heart and action to correspond with the inward working of the Holy Spirit and so to grow towards purity of heart and an abiding sense of the presence of God.

3. The monks follow in the footsteps of those whom God has, in times past, called into the desert to engage in spiritual warfare. As citizens of heaven, they become strangers to worldly ways. In solitude and silence they seek that interior quiet which gives birth to wisdom. They deny themselves in order to follow Christ. Through humility and obedience they struggle with the pride and rebelliousness of sin. Through their simplicity and labor they seek that blessedness which is promised to the poor. Through their joyful hospitality they share with their fellow pilgrims something of the peace and hope which come from Christ.

4. The monastery is an image of the mystery of the Church. Nothing is preferred to the praise of the Father's glory, and every effort is made so to conform all the details of communal life to the supreme law of the Gospel that the community is lacking in no spiritual gift. The monks are concerned to remain in harmony with the whole people of God and share in its active desire for the unity of

the Church, for it is in fidelity to the monastic way of life and its own hidden mode of apostolic fruitfulness that monks serve the people of God and the whole human race. Each community and all the monks are dedicated to Blessed Mary, the Mother and Type of the Church in the order of faith and love and perfect union with Christ.

5. The organization of the monastery is entirely directed to bringing the monks into close union with Christ, since it is only by means of a deep personal devotion to the Lord Jesus that the specific characteristics of the Cistercian vocation are realized. It is only when the brothers prefer nothing whatever to the love of Christ that they are able to find contentment and persevere in a life which is ordinary, obscure and laborious. And may he lead them all into eternal life.

Cst 4. The Character of the Order

1. Cistercian communities scattered all over the world are united in the bond of charity. Through this communion they are able to help one another in coming to a fuller understanding of their common patrimony and in putting it into practice, as well as to offer one another encouragement and assistance in times of difficulty.

2. This communion takes juridical form in the organization of the Order according to the *Charter of Charity*, interpreted by the norms of the present Constitutions. The abbots and abbesses, assembled in two interdependent Chapters, exercise a common solicitude for all the communities of the Order in matters both human and divine. This pastoral responsibility has been exercised traditionally through the institutions of filiation, visitation and the General Chapter. In addition, other organs of dialogue, collaboration and mutual service have developed by which the communion of the whole Order is fostered and the intentions of the founders are effectively adapted to modern conditions.

3. Cistercian communities, wherever they are, have one charity, one rule and similar observances. It is for each community, in dialogue with other communities, to find new ways in which the patrimony of the Order can be dynamically expressed in its own culture and according to its particular circumstances, observing always the guidelines established by the General Chapter.

Bibliography

Benedict of Nursia, *The Rule of St. Benedict 1980* (Collegeville: The Liturgical Press, 1980).

Cistercian Fathers Series, E. Rozanne Elder et al., ed. (Spencer, Mass./Kalamazoo: Cistercian Publications, 1970—).

Cistercian Studies Series, E. Rozanne Elder et al., ed. (Spencer, Mass./Kalamazoo: Cistercian Publications, 1969—).

Cummings, Charles, *Monastic Practices* (Kalamazoo: Cistercian Publications, 1986).

Hart, Patrick, ed., *The Message of Thomas Merton* (Kalamazoo: Cistercian Publications, 1981).

Leclercq, Jean, *Bernard of Clairvaux and the Cistercian Spirit* (Kalamazoo: Cistercian Publications, 1976).

Lekai, Louis J., *The Cistercians. Ideals and Reality* (Kent, Ohio: Kent State University Press, 1977).

Louf, Andre, *The Cistercian Way* (Kalamazoo: Cistercian Publications, 1980).

Merton, Thomas, *The Waters of Siloe* (New York: Harcourt Brace Jovanovich, 1949).

 The Sign of Jonas (New York: Harcourt Brace Jovanovich, 1953).

Merton, Thomas, trans. and ed., *The Spirit of Simplicity. Characteristic of the Cistercian Order* (Trappist, Ky.: Gethsemani, 1948).

Pennington, M. Basil, *Monastery: Prayer, Work, Community* (San Francisco: Harper and Row, 1983).

 Jubilee. A Monk's Journal (New York: Paulist, 1981).

 The Last of the Fathers. The Cistercian Fathers of the Twelfth Century. A Collection of Essays (Still River, Mass.: St. Bede's, 1983).

Cistercian Monasteries Today

There are today some three hundred monasteries of monks and nuns following the Cistercian way. For historical reasons, they are divided into two "Orders": the Order of Cîteaux and the Cistercian Order of the Strict Observance (sometimes called "Trappists"). Visits may be arranged with the guestmaster/guestmistress of each house and additional information obtained on the life by writing to the vocation director.

The following monasteries are located in English-speaking areas:

■   *Order of Cîteaux*
●   *Strict Observance*

★   *Monks*
♦   *Nuns*

The United States and Canada

● ★St. Joseph's Abbey
Spencer, Massachusetts
01562

● ♦ Mount St. Mary's Abbey
Wrentham, Massachusetts
02093

■ ★ Cistercian Monastery
Mount Laurel Road
Mount Laurel, New Jersey
08054

● ★ Genesee Abbey
River Road
Piffard, New York 14533

■ ★ Monastery of St. Mary
Route 1
New Ringgold, Pennsylvania
17960

● ★ Holy Cross Abbey
Route 2, Box 253
Berryville, Virginia 22611

● ★ Our Lady of Mepkin Abbey
Route 3, Box 800
Moncks Corner, South Carolina
29461

● ★ Holy Spirit Abbey
2625 Highway 212 S.W.
Conyers, Georgia 30208

● ★ Gethsemani Abbey
Trappist, Kentucky 40073

● ★ New Melleray Abbey
Dubuque, Iowa 52001

● ◆ Our Lady of the
Mississippi Abbey
Dubuque, Iowa 52001

■ ★ Our Lady of Springbank Abbey
Box 159 Rt. 3
Sparta, Wisconsin 54656

■ ◆ Valley of Our Lady
Monastery
Route 1, Box 136
Prairie du Sac, Wisconsin
53578

● ★ Assumption Abbey
Route 5, Box 193
Ava, Missouri 65608

■ ★ Our Lady of Dallas Abbey
Route 2, Box 1
Irving, Texas 75062

● ★ St. Benedict's Monastery
Snowmass, Colorado 81654

● ★ Holy Trinity Abbey
Huntsville, Utah 84317

● ◆ Santa Rita Abbey
Box 97
Sonoita, Arizona 85637

● ◆ Redwoods Monastery
Whitehorn, California 95489

● ★ Abbey of New Clairvaux
P.O. Box 37
Vina, California 96092

● ★ Our Lady of Guadalupe Abbey
Box 97
Lafayette, Oregon 97127

● ★ Notre Dame du Calvaire
Route 3
Rogersville, New Brunswick
E0A 2T0

● ◆ Notre-Dame de l'Assomption
de l'Acadie
Rogersville, New Brunswick
E0A 2T0

● ◆ Notre-Dame de Bon Conseil
Saint Romuald,
C. Lévis, Québec
G6V 6V4

● ★ Notre-Dame du Lac
1600, St.-Isidore, R.R.1
Oka, Québec
J0N 1E0

● ★ Notre-Dame de Mistassini
100 route des Trappistes
Mistassini, Québec
G0W 2C0

■ ★ Notre Dame de Nazareth
C.P. 99
Rougemont, Québec
J0L 1M0

● ★ Cistercian Monastery of
Notre Dame
Route 5
Orangeville, Ontario
L9W 2Z2

● ★ Our Lady of the Prairies
Box 310
Holland, Manitoba
R0G 0X0

Ireland

● ★Mount Melleray Abbey
   Cappoquin, Co. Waterford

● ♦Saint Mary's Abbey
   Glencairn, Co. Waterford

● ★Mount St. Joseph Abbey
   Roscrea, Co. Tipperary

● ★Mellifont Abbey
   Collon, Co. Louth

● ★Bolton Abbey
   Moone, Athy, Co. Kildare

● ★Bethlehem Abbey
   11 Ballymena Road
   Portglenone, Ballymena,
   Co. Antrim
   (Northern Ireland) BT44 8BL

Oceania

● ★Southern Star Abbey
   Kopua, Takapau
   Hawkes Bay,
   New Zealand

● ★Tarrawarra Abbey
   Yarra Glen,
   Victoria 3775
   Australia

Africa

● ★Our Lady of Victory Abbey
   P.O. Box 40
   Kipelion, Kenya

● ♦Our Lady of Praise
   Butende
   P.O. Box 660
   Masaka, Uganda

● ★Cistercian Abbey
   P.O. Box 101
   Mankon-Bamenda,
   North West Province
   United Republic of Cameroon
   (West Africa)

● ★Mount Calvary Monastery
   Awhum
   P.O. Box 698
   Enugu, Nigeria

● ♦Saint Justina Monastery
   P.O. Box 53
   Abakaliki, Anambra State
   Nigeria

■ ★Monastero dell'Assunta
   Casella post. 260
   Asmara, Ethiopia

■ ★Monastero Cisterciense
   Sub Post Office
   Mendida, per Debré Berhan
   Ethiopia

■ ★Cistercian Monastery
   P.O. Box 21902
   Addis Ababa
   Ethiopia

Great Britain

● ★Mount St. Bernard Abbey
Coalville, Leicester LE6 3UL
(England)

● ◆Holy Cross Abbey
Whitland
Dyfed
South Wales SA34 OQX

● ★Caldey Abbey
Caldey Island, off Tenby
Dyfed SA 70 7UH
(Wales)

● ★Sancta Maria Abbey
Nunraw, Haddington
East Lothian EH41 4LW
(Scotland)

● ★Our Lady of Joy Monastery
Lantao Island
P.O. Box 5
Peng Chau
Hong Kong

The following English houses belong to the Order of Bernardine Cistercian nuns:

Monastery of Our Lady of the
Sacred Heart
St. Bernard's Convent
Slough, Berks SL3 7AF

Monastery of Our Lady of
Good Counsel
St. Bernard's Convent
Westcliff-on-Sea, Essex SS0 7JS

Monastery of Our Lady of the
Visitation
St. Bernard's Priory
Hyning
Warton, Carnforth, Lancs. LA5 9SE

The following two houses belong to the Church of England:

★ Our Lady of West Malling
Abbey
Ewell Monastery
West Malling,
Kent ME19 6HH

◆ The House of Prayer
Britwell Road
Burnham, Bucks. SL1 8DQ